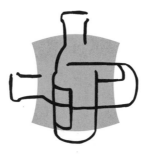

illustrations by
PAT HILLIARD-BARRY

P

THE INTERNATIONAL ANTRY COOKBOOK

by
HEIDI HAUGHY CUSICK

an **EVERYDAY GUIDE** *to cooking with* **SEASONINGS,**
prepared **SAUCES,** *and* **SPICES**

CHRONICLE BOOKS
SAN FRANCISCO

Text copyright © 1998 by Heidi Haughy Cusick. Illustrations copyright © 1998 by Pat Hilliard-Barry
Printed in the United States of America.

Design and typesetting by studio blue, Chicago

Distributed in Canada by
Raincoast Books
8680 Cambie Street
Vancouver, British Columbia
V6P 6M9

Library of Congress Cataloging-in-Publication Data:

Cusick, Heidi Haughy. The international pantry cookbook: an everyday guide to cooking with seasonings, prepared sauces, and spices/by Heidi Haughy Cusick; illustrations by Pat Hilliard-Barry.
p. cm.
Includes bibliographical references and index.
ISBN 0-8118-1670-2 (pbk.)
1. Cookery, International. 2. Sauces.
3. Spices. 4. Quick and easy cookery.
I. Title.
TX725.A1C87 1998
641.59—dc21   97-10549
                    CIP

10 9 8 7 6 5 4 3 2 1

Chronicle Books
85 Second Street, San Francisco, California 94105

Web Site: www.chronbooks.com

TABLE OF CONTENTS

1

PART ONE: AN INTERNATIONAL PANTRY

INTRODUCTION

Just inside my kitchen door is a wall furrowed with shelves from floor to ceiling. For years, in addition to every spice and herb on the market, this pantry was stocked with seasonings from all over the world, such as dried chiles, Szechuan peppercorns, annatto seeds, powdered *habanero*, dried tangerine peel, sesame seeds, tamari, and Chinese hot oil. Several times a week I combined herb leaves, spice seeds, and other ingredients and spent hours simmering sauces for an Indian curry, a Mexican mole, an Italian Bolognese.

My international larder got stocked when I was teaching a series of cooking classes for the local community college. The courses were called Cultural Foods of the World. Four nine-week classes included an hour lecture on culture and cuisine, followed by hands-on preparation of dishes from Europe, the Middle East, Asia, and the Americas. Teaching this series meant searching out the classic dishes of a country or region and interpreting them with authentic tastes.

While some of the ingredients mentioned above are still on my shelves, many are rapidly being replaced by a new generation of commercially prepared sauces, condiments, and ready-to-use seasoning blends. Natural ingredients, bold flavors, and concentrated essences make these the ultimate in convenience food. Now that someone else is spending hours blending and simmering, I can combine the results with rice, pasta, fish, meat, or vegetables in as little time as it takes to open a jar. And each day a different international cuisine is at my fingertips.

All over the world the staples — grains, meat, poultry, and vegetables — are similar. What distinguishes a regional cuisine are spices, sauces, pastes, and peppers. With the influx of packaged and bottled sauces and seasonings, previously labor-intensive dishes take a fraction of the original time. And the best part is the kitchen stays clean.

Take this from someone who was a fanatic when it came to making dinner. Every night I started from scratch. My convenience foods were tubes of tomato paste, jars of roasted red peppers, and cans of garbanzos and red beans. These plus tomatoes in puree and the occasional packet of taco seasoning were about as far as I stretched opening cans or packages.

When I visited my sisters they made fun of me and showed me how easy it is to make dinner from the freezer or a box. But I turned up my nose at the sterile flavors and salty tastes. Things began to change when I, like most people, found myself with less and less time to spend in the kitchen. I also started noticing the number of prepared sauces proliferating at the supermarket. And I couldn't ignore the variety of condiments being offered by mail order companies such as American Spoon, Dean & DeLuca, Silver Palate, Balducci's, Carol Hall's Hot Pepper Jelly, and Coyote Cafe.

One night when I was going out I wanted to make a quick pizza for the kids and bought my first Italian pasta sauce. It tasted too sweet to me, so I doctored it with wine and a can of tomato sauce. I subsequently tried other brands until I found a few that had the kind of depth and balance that took hours to make at home. Then, one wintery day, I opened a pasta sauce from Trader Joe's with chunks of fresh-tasting tomatoes and herbs and I was hooked. There was no way I could create that kind of fresh tomato flavor in December. At the same time I started paying attention to the number of beautifully packaged curry sauces, mustards, chutneys, seasoning pastes, pestos, salsas, flavored vinegars, infused oils, and preserved vegetables being stocked on grocery shelves in increasing quantities. Extraordinary packaging and appealing colors and ingredients make many of the products perfect hostess gifts and holiday presents.

Trying them became an adventure. Many times when I was browsing the international selections at a deli or supermarket, someone asked aloud, What do you do with all these products? The more of them I used, I realized the question is not what to do with them, but what did we do without them? Today there are imported and domestic products to create every ethnic cuisine imaginable (and many dishes so original they were never before contemplated!). The best ones are made with natural ingredients, seasoned purely with spices and herbs. From reading the labels I learn which products are as healthful as cooking from scratch.

Talking with other people I realized that using some of the sauces and seasonings is a challenge for a lot of people. The universal complaint I heard was that, after the jar or bottle is opened and a spoonful used, it is often stored in the refrigerator or on the shelf until mold grows and it is thrown out. Looking in my own larder made me realize I had done the same thing. So I started writing down what I did with a sauce or a condiment and sharing the ideas with friends. They in turn confided how to use their favorite products. I wrote to the producers and asked for their recommendations.

Having the flavors of the world at your fingertips is one advantage to using these products. Another is the time saved because someone else reduced stock to a flavorful essence, combed a myriad of curry paste ingredients to a brilliant paste, or cooked the marinara sauce to a richness it would take you hours to attain.

At my house I have favorite herb blends — especially ones with pieces of dried garlic and onion like those made by McFadden Farms in Mendocino County. Once I find a sauce I like, I find myself reaching for the same brand of pasta sauce, curry paste, or Mexican salsa. After a while the flavors of a product begin to feel like they are my own.

I invite you to read on and discover the possibilities for stocking your own international pantry.

INTERNATIONAL PANTRY

You are about to step into your kitchen to find the same vegetables, pasta, rice, poultry, meat, and seafood you cook day after day transformed into something special. The exotic, complex, and bold seasonings of the world, such as tapenade and pesto from Italy; fish sauces and curry pastes from Thailand; vindaloo sauce from India; barbecue rubs from the United States and the Caribbean; ground chiles from Ethiopia, Louisiana, and Jamaica; and herb blends evoking the cuisines of Mexico, Italy, Provence, or Louisiana are at your fingertips.

In the three parts of this book you'll find a description of ingredients, recipes showing the quickest ways to use them, and a guide to panaceas and quantities.

PART ONE describes commercially produced spices, sauces, pastes, condiments, and preserves. Under each heading you will find a list of ingredients that are commonly found in the product and some of the best ways to use it. Because there are so many sauces from Asia and Latin America, they have their own section. For Middle Eastern ingredients such as tahini, harissa, and ajvar, or Caribbean sauces and seasonings, look under Pastes and Pestos; Blends and Rubs; Hot Sauces; or Barbecue

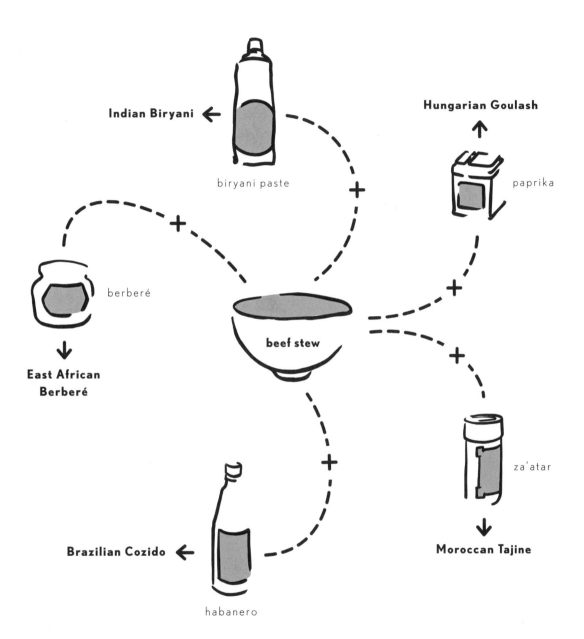

Indian Biryani ←

biryani paste

Hungarian Goulash ↑

paprika

+

+

berberé

beef stew

+

East African Berberé ↓

+

za'atar

Moroccan Tajine ↓

Brazilian Cozido ←

+

habanero

Sauces, Marinades, and Glazes. Where I think it is appropriate, I included a basic recipe to make your own chutney, mustard, salsa, or infused vinegar. Reading the recipe also gives a sense of what goes into the preparation of these condiments, so you know what to expect when you buy one.

In **PART TWO** are the recipes, drawn from classic preparations and original creations. Presented by categories from soups and salads to vegetables, breads, seafood and meat, they are uncomplicated and can be made in a matter of minutes. In the beginning of each section are master recipes. These recipes list a basic cooking method followed by variations on the master recipe with specific sauce or condiment recommendations to accommodate a specific flavor or cuisine. For example, a master recipe for Tomato Soup is followed by Spicy, Sweet and Garlicky, Mexican, African Peanut, Hungarian, and Gazpacho variations. They use pantry-stocked ingredients such as garlic paste and prepared sauces and seasoning mixtures. Think of them as suggestions. Every time I go to the store, it seems like another line of seasonings or condiments is being introduced. These recipes are recommendations; experiment and find your favorite additions.

The recipes often offer very general guidelines for the type of sauce or seasoning to use. My intention is to introduce the possibilities and entice you to taste and experiment. Some recipes are designed to bowl you over with their bold flavors. Others simply accent a dish with an exotic taste. When garlic is called for, I have almost always included the equivalent measurement for garlic paste, also known as crushed garlic and garlic puree.

What happens when you get a sauce and the flavor is not what you like? In **PART THREE** I've compiled useful information. This section includes a guide to cooking terms and techniques. Finally, a list of mail order sources makes stocking your international pantry as convenient as a phone call.

1

AN INTERNATIONAL
PANTRY

CARIBBEAN:
Achiote, allspice, avocado, casareep, cassava (yucca), coconut, coriander/cilantro, curry, dried salted fish, garlic, ginger, habanero and other chiles, hot sauces, jerk seasoning, limes, mango hot sauces, papaya hot sauces, pickled fish, rum, tropical fruits, West Indian Worcestershire, yams.

INGREDIENTS FOR CHARACTERISTIC
REGIONAL FLAVORS

Here are the ingredients that are used abundantly in these regions. To make a dish resemble the flavors you remember from your travels or simply to add a regional accent to everyday rice or chicken, choose an appealing combination and enjoy.

CREOLE:
Bell pepper, cayenne, chiles, crawfish, dried shrimp, filé powder, gulf fish, hot sauce, onions, parsley, pepper jellies, rice, tomato.

LATIN AMERICAN:
Achiote, annatto, avocado, beans, cassava (yucca), chiles, chimichurri, coconut, coriander/cilantro, corn, cumin, dried shrimp, epazote, garlic, lemon, lime, masa, mole, onions, salsa, tomato, tortillas.

MIDDLE EASTERN:

Ajvar, almonds, capers, cardamom, cinnamon, coriander/cilantro, couscous, dill, dried fruits, falafel, garlic, harissa, lentils, mint, olive oil, orange flower water, pine nuts, pomegranate, poppy seeds, preserved lemons, raisins, saffron, tahini, turmeric, walnuts, za'atar.

MEDITERRANEAN:

Basil, dried tomatoes, fennel, garlic, garlic mayonnaise, lavender, olive oil, olives, olive salads, oregano, pasta, pine nuts, red pepper relish, red pepper spread, rosemary, seafood, tapenade.

ASIAN:

Bean paste, chile paste with garlic, Chinese mustard, chutneys, coriander/cilantro, cumin, curries, curry leaves, dried fish, five-spice powder, galangal, garlic, ginger, hoisin, hot oil, kaffir lime, lemon grass, lily buds, mirin, oyster sauce, plum sauce, rice vinegar, salted black beans, salted plums, sambals, sea vegetables, sesame seeds and oil, silver and gold leaf, soy sauces, tamarind, tangerine peel, turmeric, wasabi, water chestnuts, watercress.

AFRICAN:

Banana condiments, berberé, black pepper, cassava (yucca), chiles, cloves, dried fish, fenugreek, flax seed, ginger, lemon, lentils, onion, peanuts, preserved lemons, preserved mangos, tomato, turmeric, yams.

THE SEASONINGS

For any commercial product, always read the **LABELS** and list of **INGREDIENTS** (listed in order by quantity) to find out what exactly is in it, as proprietary blends vary for even the most classic combination. Avoid products with salt as the first ingredient, or with MSG or other ingredients you don't stock in your own kitchen.

The pungent flavors and intricate spice blending of the sauces and pastes from Asia bring the aromas evocative of the cuisines of Thailand, China, Korea, Japan, Indonesia, Vietnam, the Philippines, and India to your table. Many of these, such as curry paste, black bean sauce, fish sauce, plum sauce, soy sauce, and chile paste with garlic, are staples in my pantry. Depending on their heat or intensity and the kind of flavor I'm in the mood for, I add a pinch or several tablespoons of one to the pan and make a quick sauce for sautéed chicken, fish, or vegetables. Their concentrated essences also add interesting dimensions to soups and stews. Also see Blends and Rubs (page 28), Hot Sauces (page 38), and Pastes and Pestos (page 47).

ADOBO

The name is used for two different sauces – one from the Philippines and one from Mexico. Philippine adobo is a sour, garlicky sauce of palm vinegar, garlic, bay leaves, and soy sauce in which chicken and pork are first soaked and then simmered until the sauce is cooked to a syrupy dark glaze. See Mexican and Latin American Sauces and Salsas (page 41) for the Mexican adobo.

BIRYANI PASTE

This cumin-rich, vinegary sauce also includes turmeric, garlic, ginger, and chiles. Use it as a marinade for meat or chicken and as a base for the stewed meat or vegetable dish of the same name.

BLACK BEAN SAUCE

Made from fermented black beans, this salty sauce adds a rich depth to stir-fries or Chinese pork dishes. Stir a few tablespoonfuls into a sauté of chicken or fish, a sauce for baked or steamed fish, or into a game ragout. Fermented black beans may be substituted; puree them in a blender or food processor if you don't want the texture.

CHILE PASTE

With or without garlic, this is a very hot blend of pureed salted and fermented chiles and oil. Use in tiny bits to give Thai-, Vietnamese-, or Indonesian-style heat to sauces for vegetables or rice. Put a dab in a dressing for a Thai noodle salad (page 107) or anywhere you want a rich complexity that doesn't come from plain fresh or crushed dried chiles.

CURRY PASTE

Curry pastes from India and Thailand come in jars and are mixtures of the usual curry blend of spices (see Blends and Rubs, page 28) plus lemon juice, garlic, and water to make them into a paste. Red, yellow, and green curry pastes for Thai dishes get their color from the chiles and other ingredients such as yellow turmeric, red tomatoes, and green cilantro and other herbs. Use curry paste to taste or according to the package directions to give authentic flavor to sauces for rice, vegetables, or meat. To stretch it into a sauce, add stock, coconut milk, yogurt, or water. The benefit of curry paste over the dry blend of curry spices is that it gives an instant depth to any dish.

DASHI

The base for a standard Japanese *udon* soup is made from dried sardines, bonito, mackerel, seaweed, and salt or sometimes from only bonito, seaweed, and salt. It comes in a dried form and you mix it with water. Stir in buckwheat noodles known as *soba* for an authentic dish.

SEASONING TIPS

If an Asian sauce is too thin, combine 2 tablespoons of cornstarch in 2 tablespoons of water and stir until dissolved. Add to 1 1/2 cups of sauce and heat just until thickened. If you want to use the sauce as a glaze, cool it before brushing on the food.

Always taste a sauce or seasoning before using it so you don't have any major surprises at serving time. Read the labels to get a sense of the proportions and ingredients in a product.

FISH SAUCE

Made in Vietnam, Cambodia, Laos, and Thailand from the liquid that comes from stacked and salted fish (usually anchovies), this ancient sauce, known as *nuoc mam* in Vietnam and *nam pla* in other parts of Southeast Asia, has many purposes. The best brands come from Phu Quoc, an island off the southern coast of Vietnam. Fish sauce doesn't taste fishy, but gives an amazing salty-tart quality to soups, marinades, and to dressings for noodle or beef salads.

HOISIN SAUCE

A soybean-based sauce, hoisin is sea-soned with garlic, chiles, and herbs for sweet-salty pungency. A tablespoon or so will accent a chicken or fish dish and give depth to a rice entrée such as Garlic and Ginger Stove-top Rice (page 151). Hoisin is also used in some Vietnamese dishes.

HOT CHILI OIL

This reddish-tinged chile-infused oil from China adds a subtle heat to noo-dles, sauces, and Chinese salads.

KIM CHEE

This sauce base is also the name of Korea's famous pickled cabbage dish. The crushed red chile and vinegar paste can be used to taste in a pot of cooked cabbage or wherever you want to add its distinctive spicy tartness.

KUNG PAO SAUCE

This peppery rich sauce from Szechuan, China, is used in small amounts to deglaze the pans of sautéed chicken or fish to make a pan sauce. A tablespoon or so of Kung Pao sauce in a broth or pot of beans imparts exotic flavor.

MIRIN

Concentrated sweet rice wine, mirin gives body to otherwise thin sauces and a touch of sweetness to sauces when used in small quantities.

MISO

Used in Japanese and northern Chinese cooking. The dark paste made from fermented soybeans has a con-centrated, somewhat earthy flavor, and is quite salty. Often mixed with rice or barley, the paste ferments from one to three years. It is high in vitamin B-12 and is rich in enzymes and digestive aids. Miso comes in a variety of colors and textures depending on its other ingredients and makes a nutritious soup base when used in small quanti-ties. Stirring a tablespoon or so of miso into stews, vegetables sautés, or other sauces will give a salty depth not achieved with salt alone.

OYSTER SAUCE

Despite its name, this sauce made from the essence of oyster plus soy sauce and other ingredients is not at all "fishy." Use it to season an Asian sauté of vegetables, seafood, chicken, or noodles.

PEANUT SAUCE

makes about 3/4 cup

1/4 cup soy sauce

2 tablespoons molasses

3 garlic cloves, minced, or 1 1/2 teaspoons garlic paste

1/4 to 3/4 teaspoon chile paste

2 to 3 tablespoons fresh lemon or lime juice

1/2 cup water

1/3 cup creamy peanut butter

Combine all the ingredients in a small saucepan and bring to a boil. Reduce the heat and simmer 5 minutes to blend flavors. Cool.

PEANUT SAUCE

Used in Thai and Indonesian cooking, peanut sauce dispenses a distinguishable flavor and is the signature ingredient in the popular Indonesian satay. Soy-sauce based, with the texture and aroma of peanuts, garlic, and chiles, it is used as a dipping sauce with grilled meats or raw vegetables and is equally good in a pan of sautéed vegetables, meats, and fish. You'll find it in liquid form in bottles or in packets of dried seasonings. Flavor varies dramatically from one brand to the next, so taste until you find your favorite.

PLUM SAUCE

The essence of plums comes through in the best versions of this sweet-tart sauce. It is classically served with Peking Duck and on pancakes with Mu Shu Pork (see Mu Shu-style Crêpes, page 238). I also like to put a few tablespoons in a pork stew or a homemade barbecue sauce.

SAMBAL

In Indonesia, sambals are pastes of garlic, chiles, coconut, and onions to add to other sauces. On the Indian table, they are the accompanying sauces and condiments.

SESAME OIL

The sesame seed's nutty fragrance is captured by pressing the oil from the seeds. The oil is made from either plain or toasted sesame seeds. The toasted sesame oil has the most flavor. Use both sparingly because they are expensive and because a little goes a long way.

SOY SAUCE

Soybeans fermented with wheat in salt and water produce this salty dark brown seasoning sauce that has about one-eighth the amount of sodium compared to an equivalent amount of salt. Light soy sauce has further reduced the sodium content. *Shoyu* is the Japanese word for soy sauce. Also see Tamari, page 24.

SWEET-AND-SOUR SAUCE

A northern Chinese specialty, the tart-sweetness of this sauce should be in harmony so one doesn't overpower the other. Finding a brand you like is possible only through trial and error as there are many domestic and imported sauces on the market.

SWEET-AND-SOUR SAUCE

makes about ³/4 cup

1/3 cup sugar

1/4 cup ketchup

2 tablespoons rice wine or sherry

2 tablespoons distilled white or rice vinegar

1/4 cup soy sauce

1 tablespoon cornstarch mixed with 1/3 cup water

Combine all the ingredients in a bowl and mix well. Use to deglaze pans of fried chicken, pork, or fish.

STIR-FRY SAUCE

makes about 1 1/4 cups

1/2 cup soy sauce

1/4 cup dry sherry or rice wine

1 teaspoon chopped peeled ginger or 1 1/2 teaspoons ground ginger

1 small garlic clove, minced, or 1/4 teaspoon garlic paste

1 tablespoon rice wine vinegar

2 to 3 teaspoons hoisin sauce

2 tablespoons cornstarch dissolved in 1/2 cup water

Combine all of the ingredients in a bowl. To use for stir-frying, leave out the cornstarch until ready to cook, pour half the sauce over 1 pound chicken or fish, and marinate for 15 to 30 minutes. Stir the cornstarch mixture into the remaining sauce and add to the stir-fry in the wok after you have browned the meat or fish. Cook until just thickened. To use it for coating meat for the oven or barbecue, combine all the ingredients in a saucepan and boil for 1 minute. Cool before coating the food.

STIR-FRY SAUCE

Different brands have proprietary combinations of soy sauce, ginger, sesame oil, sherry, and other ingredients, so trying them is the only way to find your favorites. Find those without MSG or too much salt for the best results. Adding a few tablespoons to a pan of bean sprouts or fried rice evokes the aromas previously found an ocean away. Use small amounts for chicken and fish and increase the quantity for beef and pork.

SZECHUAN SAUCE

This hot-sweet-salty sauce characterizes the bold flavors of Szechuan, an inland Chinese province. Ingredients include soy sauce, vinegar, garlic, a dab of sesame oil or paste, garlic, and a shot of chiles. Look for those thickened with fruit concentrates and arrowroot. Use sparingly at first and increase the amount to suit your taste in stir-fries or chicken sautés or over rice. To make your own add 1/2 to 1 teaspoon of chili paste with garlic to the stir-fry sauce preceding.

TAMARI SAUCE

Tamari is the liquid drawn off fermented miso paste. It has a darker color and slightly richer flavor and texture than soy sauce. Traditional tamari is made without wheat (read the label). Use as you would soy sauce.

TERIYAKI SAUCE

Japanese for "shining broil," teriyaki is a blend of soy sauce, mirin, and rice wine (sake), plus garlic, ginger, and other proprietorial ingredients added by each producer. It creates a classic mahogany glaze on meats, fish, and chicken.

VINDALOO

Hotter than curry dishes, vindaloo comes from the southwest coast of India, where chicken or lamb are marinated in a spicy vinegar mixture. The paste or dry seasoning mixture typically includes ground chiles, cumin, turmeric, mustard, coriander, ginger, salt, and is thinned with vinegar.

WASABI

Whether you mix your own wasabi from the green powder made from Japanese horseradish or buy it premixed and packaged in a tube, wasabi's fiery flavor gives sushi one of its distinguishing flavors. Go easy when using it, as its pastel color is deceiving. It is very hot. You can also add it sparingly to give heat to avocado and cilantro dips, or whenever you want to spike up a dish with its unique flavor.

TERIYAKI SAUCE

makes about 1 cup

$1/2$ **cup soy sauce**

$1/2$ **cup mirin** (see page 21)

$1/4$ **cup rice wine or sake**

Optional additions: 1 teaspoon chopped peeled ginger, 1 minced garlic clove or $1/2$ teaspoon garlic paste, 1 teaspoon sugar

Combine all the ingredients in a small saucepan. Bring to a boil and boil for 1 minute. Cool. Dip fillets of beef, boneless breasts of chicken, or fillets of fish in the sauce. Panfry or sauté, using all the sauce to coat the meat, until finished to a sheen. If you want to use it to coat food to be cooked in the oven, add 1 tablespoon cornstarch mixed with 2 tablespoons water to the ingredients in the saucepan and proceed with the directions for cooking.

This growing category of sauces encompasses jars and bottles of spicy, sweet, smoky, red, bronze, and golden marinades, soaks, and bastes. Most are based on tomatoes – many ketchup-style – with an incredible range of flavors.

Around the United States, specifically flavored barbecue sauces have regional appeal. For example, in South Carolina you find sauces based on mustard and on mustard and ketchup. Red sauces in varying degrees of heat and sweetness typify Kansas City, Chicago, and Tennessee barbecue. North Carolina likes a vinegar-spiked sauce, as does Texas for a beef barbecue. A mahogany-colored sauce is favored for Texas brisket, and bronze sauces are pure Mississippi rib-style. Then, there are individual producers' interpretations of sauces for the barbecue. With names like Bone Suckin' Sauce, Thunder Bay's Wild Beasty Sauce, Sweet William's Hot 'n' Nasty Bar-b-que, Crazy Jerry's A Lotta Bull Sauce, and Spicy Jones' Hot Grilling Sauce, American barbecue sauces live up to their frontier heritage.

Since cooking over coals isn't limited to the United States, interpretations of sauces and seasonings from around the world are increasingly available, some straight from the source. You'll find barbecue sauces labeled Thai, Chinese, Bol Goki (Korean), Caribbean, teriyaki, and jerk, as well as a couple of brands featuring Aussie-style blends.

Some sauces and marinades include liquid smoke, which means you could put them on food for the oven and still have a smoky flavor. Every year another batch of hot, sweet, and spiced sauces come on the market. As a lover of barbecuing, I use them as sandwich spreads and meat loaf toppings, stirred in pots of beans, and as a condiment for anything that comes off the grill as well as for sautéed hamburgers, chicken, fish, and garden burgers. Meat for the grill is only a sponge for the amazing marinades on the market.

Glazes are used for food to be grilled or broiled. Usually quite intense in their flavor, they can be brushed on just before cooking or thinned as a marinade for several hours or overnight.

BARBECUE SAUCE

makes about 1 cup

1 cup ketchup

1/2 **onion**, chopped (optional)

2 **garlic cloves** or 1 teaspoon garlic paste

2 **teaspoons soy sauce**

1 **teaspoon Worcestershire sauce**

2 **tablespoons vinegar**

2 **tablespoons brown sugar**

1/4 **teaspoon ground cloves** (optional)

Mix all the ingredients in a saucepan and bring to a boil. Reduce the heat to medium and simmer to blend flavors, about 15 minutes. Cool before using.

Herb and spice blends, once limited to Italian herbs, fines herbes, and herbes de Provence, are getting more and more specific with such names as Herbs for Glorious Goulash, Seafood Blend, Mexican Herbs, Middle East Blend, and Beaujolais Blend. While garlic powder has been a common ingredient in some blends, seek those blends with bits of dried garlic or onion for richer flavors. Avoid any in which salt is the first or major ingredient.

Some blends of dried spices and herbs give a specific taste to curry, chili, fajitas, Cajun dishes, stir-fries, or marinades.

Rubs are also blends, but they come both dry or wet from oil, wine, water, or other liquid. In either form, they are rubbed or brushed onto food for the grill, oven, or broiler. Spice blends known as rubs often contain paprika (good for browning), garlic, powdered chiles, and salt. Use a favorite blend when sautéing onions for a meat sauce, soup, or pot of beans. Use them to rub into meat or fish when grilling, broiling, baking, or sautéing. They are also excellent to sprinkle on bread or on top of mashed or scalloped potatoes. Listed with the following most commonly found blends and rubs are their characteristic seasonings and suggestions on how to use each.

BEAN BLEND

Garlic, cumin, oregano, marjoram, coriander, and dried onions are most commonly included in this blend. Epazote, a Mexican herb that is often cooked in a pot of beans, is also a possibility. Use bean blend in the sauce for a pot of beans, but as with any blend, if you like its taste, add it also to other hearty dishes such as meat stews or barbecue sauces.

BERBERÉ

This is an East African blend of paprika, cayenne, ginger, savory, basil, cumin, turmeric, allspice, cinnamon, dry mustard, coriander, cloves, and salt. Use it to spike stews or as a seasoning rub on food for the barbecue.

BOUQUET GARNI

In France, this traditional blend includes thyme, parsley, and bay leaf. Use it to flavor stocks and stews. Tie the herbs in a piece of cheesecloth if you want to keep the broth clear.

CHILI POWDER

Ground dried chiles are combined with other spices such as cumin, garlic, and salt to make a blend that gives flavor to pots of chili. Add to taco meats or Mexican rice sauces. It is milder than pure ground chiles such as cayenne.

CREOLE AND CAJUN BLENDS

Two spices you can count on in either of these blends are ground red chile and salt. In addition, such blends might include garlic, onion, paprika, sage, and mustard. Taste and use sparingly since they can be quite hot. The blackened seasoning made famous by Paul Prudhomme gets its name from a cooking method – a cast iron skillet is heated until smoking, and used to sear fish or meat that has been rubbed with the seasoning (see Blackened Fish, page 167). Red spices such as paprika and cayenne tend to darken quickly, which is why they are so good for browning. With this method they actually turn black.

CURRY POWDER

Just about every cook in India has a unique blend for seasoning curries, which is why you have to purchase different brands until you find the one you like. Curries are slightly different depending on the cuisine, so look for the blends from the Indian regions such as Madras, Kashmir, New Delhi, Bombay, and Calcutta, as well as those from Thailand and the Caribbean to get close to the authentic flavor.

Thai curry blends come in red, yellow, and green, all with quite different results. The colors come from the ripeness of the chiles and the other ingredients. In India, curry blends have from three to over twenty ingredients, of which turmeric, coriander, and chiles are ubiquitous.

Caribbean curry also combines the typical spices but with less cumin and more turmeric. Use it for curried goat or chicken to give a West Indies accent.

FAJITA BLEND

Like taco and other commercial seasoning blends, the combination of seasonings for fajitas is subject to the producer's own recipe. The basics, which give a Mexican accent, include cumin, coriander, ground chile, paprika, and salt. Herbs include oregano, marjoram, and sage. Garlic, onions, and salt are also in these blends.

FINES HERBES

A blend of equal amounts of tarragon, chives, chervil, and parsley constitutes this traditional seasoning according to *Joy of Cooking*. Thyme may also be included. This blend is used in soups and in the sauces of classic French vegetable, chicken, and meat dishes.

CURRY BLEND
makes about ¼ cup

1 tablespoon cumin

1 tablespoon coriander

1 tablespoon turmeric

1 tablespoon cardamom

1 teaspoon ground ginger

1 teaspoon fenugreek

1 teaspoon ground chile

Combine all the ingredients in a bowl and mix. Before using, sauté the mixture for 10 seconds or so to bring up the oils and aromas.

FIVE-SPICE POWDER

Star anise, cinnamon, pepper, fennel, and cloves blend together in this aromatic five-spice blend used to season Chinese dishes. I have, however, found proprietary combinations with such additional ingredients as ginger, orange peel, and licorice.

GARAM MASALA

Fifty-six spices are used in India for seasoning, says Ranjan K. Dey, proprietor of New World Spices in San Francisco. When two or more are mixed together they are known as garam masala. Each blend is created to give a particular flavor to a dish. Spices you can expect to find in the blends include cumin, fennel, cardamom, cloves, cinnamon, mace, saffron, nutmeg, turmeric, ginger, and ground chile. Turmeric gives the yellow color characteristic of curry.

GARLIC BLEND

Adding dried garlic or garlic powder to an herb blend means one less step to seasoning if you are used to peeling and chopping fresh garlic. I look for products that have little or no salt. Ones with salt limit their use and your ability to adjust the saltiness of a recipe. With garlic blends, garlic bread is easier to make than it is with fresh garlic.

HERBES DE PROVENCE

Herbs that grow in the Provençal hills are enhanced by lavender, the characteristic addition to this aromatic blend. The combination includes basil, savory, thyme, rosemary, fennel, and lavender flowers. I put it in my chicken stock pot and use it to season coq au vin and the poaching liquid for fish.

ITALIAN BLEND

Personalized blends of Italy's favorite herbs include oregano, basil, marjoram, thyme, savory, rosemary, and sage. If you have to have one herb blend in the pantry, this is the best for seasoning anything from stocks to potatoes, salads to pastas.

JERK SEASONING

Distinguished by allspice, green onions, chiles, and a selection of herbs native to Jamaica, this fiery paste can be thinned with water, wine, or coconut milk. It is the sauce of the Maroons, runaway slaves in Jamaica who learned from the native Arawaks about the chiles and wild herbs growing in the mountains and how to use them to season meat before smoking it. Dip or rub pork, chicken, or fish in jerk seasoning for up to overnight before grilling. Or, stir into meat loaf or spice up a dipping sauce with a tablespoon or two (even in twice-baked potatoes!).

MEXICAN BLEND

The seasonings that make a dish taste Mexican include cumin, ground chiles, oregano, garlic, onions, dried green bell pepper, and sometimes sage. Use Mexican blends or fajita and taco seasoning blends in beans, tacos, stews, and stir-fries.

MIDDLE EASTERN BLEND

Cumin, ground ginger, coriander, mint, lemon, cayenne pepper, and ground cinnamon typically impart their essence to stewed meats and vegetables around the eastern Mediterranean. In addition, sumac may be added to give its distinctive sour taste to meat dishes. The blend should be a mellow backdrop rather than a strong flavor in slow-cooked pots of food, so go easy on it.

SEAFOOD BOIL

Use this seasoning to flavor a big pot of boiling water in which you are going to cook freshly caught crab, crawfish, mussels, or clams with some vegetables. Most versions have salt and pepper with other ingredients adjusted by regional preferences. A Cajun crawfish boil blend will have plenty of cayenne pepper plus a little thyme, sage, garlic, salt, and pepper. A crab boil typically combines bay leaves, dill seed, mustard seed, coriander, allspice, salt, and black pepper.

SOUTHWESTERN BLEND

Although you'll find many versions, most Southwestern blends are similar in composition to Mexican blends. Only the product names are different.

SZECHUAN BLEND

The dried combination of garlic, onion, ginger, paprika, ground chile, and black pepper contributes a spicy backdrop when seasoning a stir-fry. You can also use this as a rub for barbecued meats.

SEASONING TIP

Stir flour into rubs and spice blends if they are too hot and you want to minimize their fiery quality when rubbing on fish or meat.

TACO SEASONING

Like a fajita blend, the formula for a taco seasoning is determined by the producer. The main ingredients are cumin, garlic, onions, coriander, oregano, and salt.

TANDOORI SPICES

A tandoor is the name of the clay oven heated with a wood fire, a popular cooking method from Punjab, in Pakistan. Meat, poultry, and bread (such as nan) cooked in this way is referred to as tandoori. You may find grilling spices to marinate the meat in a tandoori style and then you can broil or grill it as you like.

THAI SEASONING

Like taco or fajita seasoning, a Thai spice blend is a producer's intimation of the seasonings of a cuisine. Combinations most likely include ground chile, ginger, coriander, star anise, garlic, lemon grass (or lemon peel), shallots, curry leaves, and basil.

VINDALOO

See Asian Pastes and Sauces, page 19.

ZA'ATAR

This is a blend of marjoram, thyme, sumac, and salt from the Middle East, where it is typically sprinkled on pita or other flat bread before baking, and is sometimes used in meat dishes such as Moroccan Lamb Tajine (page 207).

BASIC RUB

makes about 1/4 cup

1 tablespoon paprika

1 teaspoon cayenne pepper

1 teaspoon salt

1/2 teaspoon freshly ground black pepper

1/2 teaspoon ground allspice

Dash of ground cloves (optional)

1 1/2 tablespoons garlic powder

3 tablespoons vegetable oil (optional)

In a small bowl, combine the spices (and oil, if using) and mix well. With a spoon and your fingers or a pastry brush, cover chicken parts, steaks, chops, ribs, or fish on all sides with the seasoning. Place the food in a dish and cover with plastic wrap. Refrigerate at least one hour (for fish) or up to overnight for poultry and meat.

BOUILLON AND STOCK

Ready-made bouillon and stock concentrates are a boon to those who don't have hours to simmer their own. Some excellent products, in reduced glace de viande-style, liquid form, and frozen are being produced. They taste and smell wonderful as broths and add depth to soups, deglazed pan sauces, poaching liquids, and stews. Look for those that are low or free of salt and other additives. Some are vegetarian. Others are made from chicken, beef, and veal. In the recipes, stock refers to those that are homemade and unsalted; broth is canned. Broth and stock can be used interchangeably, but broths are usually salted, so be aware of that when adding other seasonings. See Sources (page 248) for producers. See Stock (page 68) for recipes for vegetable, chicken, and beef stocks.

SEASONING TIP

If a sauce is too bland, stir in a tablespoon or so of tomato paste, pesto, red pepper spread, or olive salad for tomato sauces; and a tablespoon or so of concentrated stock such as a glace de viande (check for saltiness first) to deglazed pan sauces, gravies, or stews. For any sauce, add a tablespoon or more of a complementary spice or herb blend (without salt), especially one that has dried onions and garlic in it.

 After mustard, these are the fastest-growing group of condiments. Made from fruits, herbs, and vegetables, they add potent hits to everyday dishes from cracker and pizza toppings to soup and sandwich ingredients. Staples in my house include red pepper spread, pesto, caponata, olive salad, tapenade, and artichoke pesto, and at least two chutneys.

CAPONATA
makes about 3 cups

1 large globe eggplant, unpeeled, cut into 1/2-inch cubes

1 onion, chopped

1 green or red bell pepper, seeded and chopped

3 or 4 Roma tomatoes, chopped

1/2 cup pimento-stuffed green olives, chopped

1 tablespoon capers

4 garlic cloves, minced, or 2 teaspoons garlic paste

1/3 to 1/2 cup red wine vinegar

1/2 cup water

1 to 2 tablespoons sugar

1 tablespoon Italian herb blend

Salt and freshly ground black pepper

This recipe is adapted from one by Elisabeth Rozin in *Ethnic Cuisine.*

Combine all of the ingredients in a large nonreactive pot and mix well. Bring the mixture to a boil, reduce the heat to medium-low, and cook, partially covered, until vegetables are tender, about 20 minutes. Lower the heat; remove the cover, and continue to simmer until all the liquid is evaporated, another 20 minutes or so. Cool and store, covered, in the refrigerator for up to 1 month.

CAPONATA

Eaten as a side dish or a spread for breads, the Italian eggplant, pepper, olive, and onion mixture is a standard condiment in my house. Whether I make or buy caponata, having its tart, hearty flavors on hand means I have instant appetizers when I spread it on crackers or crostini. When mixed with a can of tomato sauce and heated, it is one of my favorite bases for pasta and polenta sauces as well as an addition to bean or vegetable soups.

CHUTNEY

makes about 2 cups

2 ripe mangos, peeled and chopped

2 onions, finely chopped

3 garlic cloves, minced, or 1 1/2 teaspoons garlic paste

1 to 2 tablespoons chopped peeled ginger

1 cup cider vinegar or white wine vinegar

1 to 2 Thai or serrano chiles, seeded and minced, or 1/2 to 2 1/2 teaspoons chile paste

1/2 cup sugar

1 teaspoon salt

1 to 2 teaspoons curry blend

1/2 cup golden raisins

1/2 cup water

Combine all the ingredients in a saucepan and bring to a boil. Lower the heat and simmer, stirring frequently, until the mixture is cooked down to a thick, shiny consistency, 30 to 40 minutes. Cool and store, covered, in the refrigerator for up to 2 months. For the best taste, wait a week after making to serve.

BALSAMIC ONION RELISH

makes about 1 cup

2 tablespoons olive oil

2 large red onions, sliced

1 tablespoon sugar

1/4 cup balsamic vinegar

Salt and freshly ground black pepper

In a nonreactive saucepan over medium heat, warm the oil. Sauté the onions with the sugar until wilted, about 4 minutes. Reduce the heat to medium-low and stir in the vinegar. Cook until the onions are very tender and all the liquid is absorbed, about 20 minutes. Add salt and pepper to taste. Cool and store, covered, in the refrigerator for up to 1 week.

CHUTNEY

The traditional base of this east Indian condiment is mango, a plump yellow fruit, used both green and ripe. Mangoes grow well in India, where chutney typically is served with curries. Chutneys are characterized by their sweet-hot flavor, which comes from combining fruit, such as mangoes or apples, pears, or even bananas, with onions, sweet and hot peppers, and vinegar. In addition to serving with curries, chutney makes a great sandwich or cracker spread. For an appetizer, put a small spoonful on an endive spear or a dollop on a cream cheese-covered cracker or crouton. A curry or any vegetable soup with some chutney stirred in is transformed.

RELISHES

Unlike a chutney, a relish isn't necessarily spicy or vinegar-flavored. The term is a loose label for a wide range of vegetable mélanges. They are classified as relishes because their ingredients are chopped in small pieces and the flavor is strong enough to stand alone on the plate next to something bland like poached fish or steamed vegetables. Relishes are perfect for sandwiches, especially the olive combinations. Some of these are called "salsa," but their texture and flavor is more like a relish, which to me means you could put them on a sandwich. Think of an onion relish such as this one for Balsamic Onions when sausage sandwiches or pizza are on your menu.

I know people who collect hot sauces because of the packaging. With names like Lucifer's Damnation, Scorned Woman, and Smokin' Oranges, an Incendiary Concoction, you get an idea of what might be inside. Some are like Tabasco, made only from chiles fermented with salt and vinegar. Others include a huge range of ingredients from mundane to exotic. Reading labels may tell you what the sauce started with, but the heat of the chiles determines the ultimate flavor. Here is a selection of the types of international hot sauces that will add authentic heat to Asian, Mexican, Caribbean, or Creole dishes.

AJVAR

A puree of chiles, peppers, and other ingredients from Morocco, ajvar comes mild (sometimes called sweet) or hot. Its thick texture and orange color make it an appealing fiery addition to many sauces, especially when served over couscous.

AMERICAN HOT SAUCES

Entertainingly labeled with attention-getting names, American-made hot sauces are pureed blends of many ingredients held together by their varying degrees of chile-rich fire. Read the labels and taste before using to determine how much to start with in a dish. Put several on the table and let everyone choose a favorite.

CARIBBEAN HOT SAUCES

Usually made with *habanero*, the hottest chile on the chart, Caribbean hot sauces have a really distinctive flavor. Use sparingly and to taste in sauces or pots of beans when you want an island-style theme. Jerk seasonings are semimoist combinations of chiles, herbs, and spices. (See Blends and Rubs, page 31.)

CHILE PASTE

See Asian Pastes and Sauces, page 190.

CHIPOTLE SAUCE

See Mexican and Latin American Sauces and Salsas, page 41.

HARISSA

This fiery paste of ground dried chiles, vegetables, olive oil, and spices such as caraway, coriander, and cumin is used in North African and Middle Eastern cooking. Taste for heat and use it to season meat, chicken, or vegetable stews served with couscous or rice.

HOT PEPPER JELLY

This high-pectin fruit jelly is infused with green or red chiles and typically serves as a condiment in Louisiana Creole and Cajun cooking. Sweet is the main flavor note, with the bite of chile in the background.

SWEET CHILI (CHILE SAUCE)

This puree of chiles is sweetened enough to mute some of the heat, leaving a refreshing aftertaste. Use it in Southeast Asian noodles or shrimp dishes, or add a dab to seafood salads.

VINEGAR-CHILE SAUCES

Two styles are made: One is vinegar infused with whole chiles inside, a table fixture in African-inspired kitchens from Senegal to Bahia, the Caribbean to the American South. The other is the thicker, Tabasco-style sauce found throughout the American South to season everything from a pot of greens to red beans and rice with its tart-hot flavor.

SEASONING TIPS

If a relish, such as red pepper, is too sweet (read labels for sugar as an ingredient!), blend in 2 to 3 pieces of roasted red bell peppers to 1/4 cup of the relish.

When adding wine to a recipe, hold back on the salt, as wine has a salty quality.

KETCHUPS

These thick sauces, usually tomato-based, that we think of only for putting on French fries, hamburgers, or — if you were my grandfather — scrambled eggs, are now being concocted from cranberries, smoked tomatoes, and other ingredients. Their untraditional flavors call for experimentation to vary the taste of sandwiches, broiled steaks, meat loaf. But try them on French fries, hamburgers, and garden or soy-based burgers too!

MAYONNAISE

Flavored with garlic, chiles, or red peppers, mayonnaise and mayonnaise-butter spreads are taking on a far-reaching culinary role. Once confined to sandwiches and artichokes, mayonnaise is now also a flavored dip and a sauce for vegetables and toasts. Even Provence's garlicky mayonnaise, once only a dip for vegetables and salt cod, is dolloped on pizza or soup (see Quick Aioli, page 121). To any mayonnaise, stir in dried or fresh herbs such as rosemary to make a sauce for braised lamb shanks, a dab of chile paste to accompany sea bass fillets, and wine or a bit of horseradish to serve with roast beef. Look for other garlicky and shelf-stable buttery spreads to quickly make garlic bread or melt over vegetables.

As more of the seasonings from Mexico and South America come north, a new world of flavors is being tasted in the United States. Most Mexican sauces include some kind of chile, but the rest of Latin America combines herbs to season dishes. In this section traditional as well as contemporary combinations are described.

ACHIOTE
See Pastes and Pestos (page 47).

ADOBO
The Mexican sauce called adobo may come as a paste or sauce and includes sesame seeds, chiles, garlic, onions, cumin, oregano, coriander, and often a thickener such as bread or bread crumbs. When chipotle chiles are packed in adobo (they come in 4-ounce cans) the mixture is spicy hot. Use similar to mole to season and thicken stews. For the Filipino version see Asian Pastes and Sauces (page 19).

CHIMICHURRI
In Latin American cooking from the Caribbean throughout South America, you'll find this paste of parsley, garlic, other herbs such as basil and sometimes citrus juice or vinegar, to season a multitude of dishes.

CHIPOTLE SAUCE
Chipotles are smoked jalapeño chiles, found dried or canned in adobo sauce, a thick puree of tomatoes, vinegar, onions, and spices. They are quite hot but have incredible depth, smoky flavor, and a dark brown color. Approach them with caution at first. Add chipotle sauce to meat sauces, dipping sauces, and pots of beans.

MOLE
A classic *mole poblano* includes several kinds of chiles such as anchos, pasillas, and mulatos, plus garlic, onions, sesame seeds, epazote, cinnamon, anise seeds, almonds, tomatoes, peppercorns, and – its characteristic ingredient – unsweetened chocolate. Thin commercial mole paste with water or stock to make a fast turkey mole. Use the paste by the spoonful in chili beans or in sauces or fillings for tacos or enchiladas.

SALSAS

Finely or coarsely chopped ingredients mixed together define a wide range of products called salsa, the Mexican word for sauce. Typically made from tomatoes, salsas now are also made from tomatillos, kiwis, Vidalia onions, mangoes, papayas, chayote, corn, avocados, and other ingredients. There are so many flavors and ranges of heat to salsas, you really have to do some research to find your favorites. The fresh ones in the deli section of supermarkets are often very good, but so are many of the products in jars. When making your own, tomatoes and chiles are what you start with, then add to your heart's content onions, garlic, oregano, cumin, cilantro, avocado, corn, beans, mango, and banana. In addition to using them as dips, with tacos, and with Mexican dishes, stir salsas into bland sauces and creamy soups to give them personality. Pass them at the table with roast chicken, ragus of beef, or pots of beans. During the summer, add diced tomatoes and chopped cilantro to commercial salsas to freshen them. Here are two starter recipes, one using ingredients from your pantry and the other using fresh tomatoes.

PANTRY SALSA

makes about 2 cups

2 cups chopped canned tomatoes

1/2 cup chopped onion

1 or 2 canned chiles or chiles in vinegar, minced, or 1 to 2 teaspoons hot sauce

1 or 2 garlic cloves, minced, or 1/2 to 1 teaspoon garlic paste (optional)

2 tablespoons fresh lime or lemon juice

Chopped fresh cilantro or parsley

Salt and freshly ground black or white pepper

Combine all the ingredients in a bowl and season to taste with salt and pepper. Adjust the heat and add whatever else you like. See Salsas, above. Tabasco or other hot sauce can be substituted for the chiles.

FRESH SALSA

makes about 2 cups

1 pound ripe tomatoes, cored and chopped (2 cups chopped)

1/2 cup chopped onion

1 or 2 fresh chiles, seeded and minced

1 or 2 garlic cloves, minced, or 1/2 to 1 teaspoon garlic paste (optional)

2 tablespoons fresh lime or lemon juice

Chopped fresh cilantro or parsley

Salt and freshly ground black or white pepper

Combine all the ingredients in a bowl and season to taste with salt and pepper. Adjust the heat and add whatever else you like. See Salsas, page 42, for suggestions.

SEASONING TIP

Stir one or two chopped fresh tomatoes into a salsa, tomato soup, or pasta sauce to bring up the fresh flavor.

From the seed of the world's oldest spice comes the preparation that started the whole condiment craze. Yellow mustard as made by Morehouse and Heinz was the most popular choice in the 1950s. Then, in the 1970s, came America's fascination with French Dijon, which gets its flavor from wine, wine vinegar, or verjus. My hometown spawned Mendocino Mustard – a hot-sweet combination – right at the beginning of the mustard craze in the early 1980s. Now mustard comes with whole seeds and is flavored with herbs, citrus, wine, garlic, chiles, horseradish, peppers, onions, chocolate – you name it! The only way to know what you like is by tasting. When cooked, the pungency in mustard tends to mellow. That's why a whole chicken can be cloaked in mustard, à la Julia Child, with divine results.

MUSTARD

makes about 1¹/3 cups

1 cup dry mustard

1 cup water

1 cup white wine vinegar, cider vinegar, or white wine

2 teaspoons sugar

2 teaspoons salt

Optional additions: ¹/4 teaspoon turmeric, 3 tablespoons whole mustard seeds, 2 garlic cloves, minced, or 1 teaspoon garlic paste, 2 to 3 tablespoons red pepper paste, 1 tablespoon minced peeled ginger

Combine all the ingredients in a saucepan and mix well. Bring to a boil, lower the heat, and simmer, stirring frequently, until the mixture is smooth and thickened, 10 to 15 minutes. Pour into a jar and let cool. Store, covered, in a cool place for up to 2 months. For the best taste, wait a week after making to serve.

PASTA SAUCES

Among the easiest sauces to make yourself are those for pasta. Nonetheless, an amazing array of chunky, smooth, thick, thin, sweet, tart, and spicy pasta sauces are the biggest category of ready-made sauces you'll find on market shelves. They are usually quite concentrated, which makes them easily stretched and therefore more economical. I keep several kinds on the shelves and have included pasta sauces in recipes in most of the chapters. From a Milanaise Rice Salad (page 99) to a quick soup (page 71) to a deglazed pan sauce for fish or chicken, pasta sauce is indispensable.

Making one from scratch, however, takes not much more time than opening a jar or can. The flavors of the commercial sauces do warrant investigation, as does coordinating a mushroom- or olive-flecked sauce with a similarly flavored pasta. See Pasta (page 146) for more ideas and suggestions.

SEASONING TIPS

To thicken sauces, try one of the following methods:

For red sauces, add 1 cup or more of a thick sauce such as enchilada or pasta sauce.

Dissolve 2 to 3 tablespoons rice flour or potato flour in $1/4$ cup of the sauce, then stir the mixture into the hot dish to help thicken it.

For stews in which clarity of the sauce doesn't matter, stir in a few tablespoons of fine dry bread crumbs.

TOMATO PASTA SAUCE

makes about 1 quart

2 tablespoons canola, safflower, or olive oil

1 onion, chopped

1 red or green bell pepper, seeded and chopped (optional)

1 carrot, grated (optional)

1 cup mushrooms, sliced (optional)

1 cup mixed vegetables, chopped (optional)

2 to 4 garlic cloves, or 1 to 2 teaspoons garlic paste

2 to 4 tablespoons fresh or dried herbs or Italian blend

One 28-ounce can (3 1/2 cups) crushed tomatoes in puree

1/2 cup red or white wine, stock, or water

Salt and freshly ground black or white pepper

In a saucepan over medium heat, warm the oil. Sauté the onion (along with any of the other vegetables you are using) until softened, 2 to 5 minutes (depending on how many ingredients are in the pan). Stir in the garlic and sauté for 20 to 30 seconds. Add the herbs, tomatoes, wine, and salt and pepper to taste. Cook over medium heat to blend flavors, about 20 minutes. The longer it cooks, the richer the flavor; the shorter the time, the fresher it will taste.

PASTES AND PESTOS

Garlic, olives, chiles, ginger, sesame seeds, tomatoes, annatto seeds, tamarind, anchovies, basil, sun-dried tomatoes, wasabi, and artichokes are all concentrated into pastes and spreads. Some come in jars, such as regular or roasted garlic paste, chile paste with garlic, sesame seed paste (tahini), olive tapenade, artichoke pesto, basil pesto, and sun-dried tomato pesto. Others, which are often used just a little at a time, including anchovy, tomato, wasabi, sun-dried tomato, and pesto pastes, come in squeezable tubes that keep them fresh for months. Pastes and pestos are the ultimate in convenience for spicing up a sauce. Here are some explained in more detail.

ACHIOTE PASTE

Made from tiny red annatto seeds with the addition of spices and garlic, achiote paste comes in a small red brick. Not hot. Use a tablespoon or so in pots of beans. Thin with vinegar, wine, or water and use to marinate meat, fish, or poultry for the barbecue. Also makes a great turkey baste. If you can't find the paste, you can make your own with the seeds. Puree them in a blender or food processor with garlic, oregano, paprika, salt and pepper, and a little oil to bind it all together.

ADOBO

For the Filipino version, see Asian Pastes and Sauces (page 19). For the Latin American type, see Mexican and Latin American Sauces and Salsas (page 41).

AJVAR

See Hot Sauces (page 38).

ANCHOVY PASTE

Comes in a tube and is useful to keep on hand for seasoning Caesar Salad dressing; for making the Provençal pizza, Pissaldière; and for seasoning the Swedish scalloped potatoes known as Jannson's Temptation. A small squirt in a salad dressing or potato soup adds the most amazing amount of depth.

CHILE PASTE

See Asian Pastes and Sauces (page 20).

CURRY PASTE

See Asian Pastes and Sauces (page 20).

GARLIC PASTE

Also called crushed garlic and garlic puree, garlic paste is fast becoming my favorite way to add garlic to any sauce. Some brands tend to be bitter or have a metallic taste, so taste them and find one you like. A roasted garlic paste is sweeter and adds a mellow garlic dimension to pizza, sautés, or canapés.

GINGER

No need to wonder about how to store fresh ginger after you've used the inch or so required for a recipe. Jars of crushed ginger and chopped ginger are great for keeping rotting ginger out of the refrigerator and soggy ginger out of the freezer. You can substitute prepared chopped or crushed ginger for the chopped or minced peeled ginger called for in any recipe. Another advantage of prepared ginger is that most of the processed commercial products are made from young stem ginger, which has the most aromatic flavor and tender texture – a major improvement to the dried out, older ginger I find in my supermarket. It's one of my favorite flavors, so I use ginger in the usual stir-fries and hot and sour soups, but I also like it in chicken or seafood sautés, sprinkled on vegetables, and in desserts. Candied ginger has a sweet, caramelized texture and taste, so use it accordingly.

JERK SEASONING

See Blends and Rubs (page 31).

MISO

See Asian Pastes and Sauces (page 21).

MOLE

See Mexican and Latin American Sauces and Salsas (page 41).

PESTO

Until recently, "pesto" referred primarily to the Italian paste made of basil leaves, garlic, olive oil, pine nuts, and grated Parmesan cheese. It is, however, now more broadly defined, with pastes made of mint, sun-dried tomatoes, cilantro, and other ingredients bearing the name. Any of them are suitable to toss with pasta, although some of them are best if diluted with stock, oil, or water. Try them dolloped on pizza, drizzled in soups, or spread on sandwiches or crackers for canapés. Sun-dried tomato pesto has a tart, concentrated tomato flavor that I like in stir-fries, baked rice, chicken stews, or fish sautés. When basil is prolific in the summer, make batches of it for the freezer. Pesto is available in jars, but the commercial frozen ones, like those made by Casa de Lisio, are best. I just cut out what I need and keep the rest frozen. To keep on hand for small squirts into soups or sauces, tubes of pesto are also on the market.

RED PEPPER SPREAD

Made from sweet red bell peppers, this is a favorite in my house, where I'll admit I put it on something several times a week. It is so versatile, there's a recipe using it in every chapter. Also labeled as sweet red pepper relish or paste, or pepperonata, it is a base for making rouille, the Provençal condiment for fish soup (see Provençal Bourride, page 87). It adds sweetness to tomato sauces, and it stands alone as a canapé topping.

TAHINI

This is a Middle Eastern name for sesame seeds ground into paste. It is the classic seasoner for baba ghanouj, an eggplant dip, and for hummus, the garbanzo bean spread. If you like sesame seeds, you'll find your own ways to use it, especially in preparations for eggplant or chicken.

TAMARIND PASTE

The viscous interior of long dark brown tamarind pods has such a tart flavor it can be used in place of lemon. Usually found in paste form, tamarind is an ingredient in some curries, and diluted in hot water, it becomes a dipping sauce for Indian samosas. It is also used in Mexico as a sauce ingredient, as a drink base in many Latin American countries, and is made into candy in some parts of Asia. Its tart flavor is a nice addition to a hot and sour soup or for deglazing a pan of sautéed fish.

PESTO

makes about 3/4 cup

2 cups packed fresh basil leaves

3 to 4 garlic cloves, minced, or 1 1/2 to 2 teaspoons garlic paste

1/2 teaspoon salt

1/2 cup olive oil

3/4 cup grated Parmesan cheese

4 tablespoons pine nuts, toasted (optional)

In a blender or food processor, puree the basil and garlic. Add all the rest of the ingredients and puree until smooth. With nuts, pesto will keep 4 to 5 days in the refrigerator; without, a week. Or freeze for up to 2 months.

RED PEPPER SPREAD

makes about 1 cup

Using fresh bell peppers gives you the option of leaving the texture chunky or pureeing the mixture into a paste. Either style is used the same way.

2 tablespoons canola, safflower, or olive oil

2 red bell peppers, seeded and finely chopped

1 to 2 shallots, finely chopped

2 to 3 garlic cloves, minced, or 1 to 1 $^1/_2$ teaspoons garlic paste

Salt and freshly ground black or white pepper

Several leaves fresh basil, chopped, or 1 teaspoon dried basil (optional)

In a small skillet over medium heat, warm the oil. Sauté the remaining ingredients except the salt, pepper, and basil, for 15 to 30 minutes, depending on how much texture you want. The longer it cooks the softer the peppers get and the more the mixture holds together. Puree if desired, or use as is. Season to taste with salt and pepper and stir in the basil (if using).

TAPENADE

Olive paste from Italy imparts the pure tang and texture of ripe, cured olives to any dish. It is a combination of olives, garlic, and olive oil blended into a paste. Use it on crostini or canapés, or stir a few tablespoons into a pasta sauce or focaccia dough. See Italian Olive Chicken Sauté (page 193) for a main dish made with tapenade. Different brands have different flavors, depending on the type and curing of the olives used.

TOMATO PASTE

In the tube, this is a handy condiment to keep in the refrigerator. Use it in salad dressings, in sauces to give tartness or a little color, or anywhere you need a small hit of tomato essence.

WASABI

See Asian Pastes and Sauces (page 25).

SEASONING TIP

To change the flavor of an olive tapenade, stir in more
olive oil, or puree olives that have a flavor you like and stir them in.
Adjust the garlic to taste.

Although one of the fastest-growing cottage-produced condiments, salad dressings, to my taste, still have a long way to go. Making them shelf stable is usually done at the expense of flavor, which loses freshness. They are, however, worth pursuing and finding favorites because they save time and encourage the eating of greens and vegetables. They are also increasingly made without fat, but excellent examples are few and far between since often sugar in the guise of fruit juice is the fat substitute.

I prefer having flavored oils and vinegars on hand, using them to make a batch of salad dressing to last a few days, and then changing the combination for the next batch. However you prefer to acquire dressings, ready-made combinations are invaluable to make Classic Potato Salad (page 103) or to toss over steamed vegetables. Some have such a concentration of flavor I mix a little in other dressings or sauces. See Salad Dressing, page 94, for a basic recipe.

VINEGARS AND OILS

Wine vinegars and olive and other oils are flavored or infused with tarragon, raspberries, spices, garlic, mustard seeds, fruit, peppercorns, and edible flowers. Flavored vinegars are made by simply combining the fresh ingredients and vinegar. Infusion is done by heating the ingredients with the vinegar or oil. Flavored products usually have a less defined taste that intensifies as they age. Vinegar and oil pick up the heat of chiles substantially. Infused vinegars and oils are more aromatic and intense. To use oil sparingly, the spray cans of vegetable and olive oils are great.

To explore the possibilities of these products, personal preference rules. Flavored oils and vinegars make quick bases for salad dressings. They also add their mark to sautés of fish, chicken, and vegetables. They are as beautiful to have on the pantry shelves as they are fun to taste in all kinds of preparations. The simpler the better, however, so their fruit, nut, or other aromas are maintained.

OLIVE OIL

Look for olive oil in three varieties: extra-virgin, virgin, and pure olive oil. Extra-virgin and virgin describe the highest grade of oil. It comes from the first pressing of ripe olives. These oils have the most fruity-rich flavors and aromas – which range from mild to peppery. Pure olive oil is a lesser grade refined oil that is mild to neutral in flavor. Use the more expensive virgin olive oil when you want the flavor to come through, such as for salads and bread, and the rest for most types of cooking.

NUT AND SEED OILS

Sesame, walnut, hazelnut, and other such oils are made by pressing the natural oil from the nuts. Most of the American-made oils have processed out the nutty aroma and flavor. See Sources (page 253) for producers of excellent nut oils.

BASIC FLAVORED VINEGAR

makes about 1 quart

I make the fruit version of this every year with raspberries and blackberries that come in profusion in my garden. Two methods are given here, one in which the vinegar is heated to help infuse it with the flavor of the herbs; the other, used mainly with fruit, is made with cold vinegar. Store the vinegar in a cool place and it will keep for a year. Its flavor intensifies with time.

1 quart white wine vinegar

2 cups fresh raspberries, blackberries, crushed peaches or **1 cup leaves and sprigs of fresh herbs such as basil, chives (and their flowers), bay leaves, and tarragon,** or **1 tablespoon black peppercorns** or **as many whole tiny chiles as you like to fill up the jar**.

HEAT METHOD In an enameled or stainless-steel saucepan, bring the vinegar to boil. Place any combination of herbs, spices, or chiles in clean jars or bottles and pour the hot vinegar over them. Cover and let steep for 4 to 5 weeks in a cool place. Strain before using, adding fresh herbs to the bottles if you like.

COLD METHOD Place the fruit in clean jars or bottles and pour the vinegar over them. Cover and let steep, preferably on a windowsill which helps infuse color, for 4 to 5 weeks. Stir the fruit occasionally. Strain before using.

TRUFFLE OIL

Imported from Italy, truffle oil is an extravagant item, but one which, when used in small quantities, adds the most aromatic infusion to pasta, potatoes, and eggs.

GRAPESEED OIL

Used for everything from frying to salad dressing, grapeseed oil is made from crushed grape seeds. It has a light flavor, somewhat like refined French olive oils. It comes in flavors such as roasted garlic, basil and garlic, chili, citrus cilantro, and ginger garlic.

VERJUS

The juice of unripened grapes is made by Californians who have access to them. The flavor is between lemon juice and vinegar. Use it to deglaze a chicken or fish sauté pan or add a splash or two wherever you need a tart counterbalance.

RICE VINEGAR

A mild vinegar found both plain and seasoned (mainly with a little sugar), rice vinegar has such a wonderful flavor. I recommend sprinkling it on lettuce or vegetables as an oil-free dressing.

SHERRY VINEGAR

This elegant condiment has the distinctive sweet-tartness of sherry, so use it to taste. It is often substituted in Chinese cooking for rice wine and rice vinegar.

HOT CHILI OIL

See Asian Pastes and Sauces (page 21).

INFUSED OLIVE OIL

makes 1 quart

Use regular olive oil for this recipe and save the virgin products and extra virgins for their own flavors. They are too expensive to infuse with other aromas.

1 quart olive oil

1 cup packed fresh leaves or sprigs of rosemary, thyme, tarragon, or basil; or crushed or fresh chiles or ginger

Heat the oil in a saucepan until just hot to the touch. Place the other ingredients in clean jars and pour the oil over them. Let steep at least a week before using. Store in a cool place for up to 2 months.

MAINSTAYS

In addition to sauces, condiments, and seasonings, I keep other ingredients in my pantry. These are the extras – such as artichoke hearts – that can be made into a dip or used to enhance a sauté. They are the bases – such as pasta, rice, and beans – upon which go all the boldly flavored sauces made from the rest of the larder. They are the ingredients – such as dried mushrooms and spray oil – that add their own conveniences to dinner. And they are my recommendations for ingredients – such as enchilada sauce and canned pumpkin, sesame seeds and Szechuan peppercorns – that don't fit in any of the other categories, but keep well and do a world of good, from thickening to seasoning and everything in between. Keep these in your pantry, and you'll never be at a loss for a complete meal.

ARTICHOKE HEARTS

Very meaty, these can go into salads, soups, chicken sautés, and on pizzas. They can also be ground into puree for dips and spreads. Stock them plain, marinated, frozen, or in all three forms.

BAY LEAF

Because of the shape, we called bay "camelia" leaves when my siblings and I picked them out of mom's stews. Bay leaf adds an earthy dimension to soups and pasta sauces and is a must in the stock pot.

BEANS

Garbanzo beans (also known as chickpeas or ceci beans), red, black, cannellini, and white beans, and black-eyed peas are filled with protein and add their own flavors and textures to soups and salads, or may be pureed as the base for dips and spreads. Stock them canned or dried. When using canned beans, drain and rinse them to remove the salty brine they are packed in. If you buy packages of mixed beans, they are best made into soups, since beans take varying amounts of time to cook. Refried beans are another pantry staple. They have multiple purposes as side dishes, fillings for burritos or omelets, or as a thickening agent for soups.

BELL PEPPERS

Roasted red and yellow bell pepper strips are handy when peppers are out of season or when you just want to quickly add their color and texture to a sauce, salad, or pizza. Plain roasted peppers can be substituted for bell peppers in any recipe. Some red peppers are called pimientos; they are usually packed in vinegar.

BREAD CRUMBS

Seasoned or plain, these give a crunchy topping to stuffed vegetables or other baked dishes and they are good for thickening sauces. To make your own, toast day-old bread in the oven at 325 degrees F until dried out. Grate or grind in a food processor until fine. Store in an airtight container or in the freezer.

CAPERS

Along with their bigger counterparts, caper berries, capers add tartness to dressings and sauces that need a particular piquancy such as Caribbean meat stews, Spanish rice dishes, Italian caponata, pizza, and Scandinavian smorgasbord fare.

CARAWAY

The dark seed gives character to rye bread, German cabbage dishes, and Eastern European potato salads.

CHILES

Dried whole, crushed, ground, canned, or made into sauce, chiles have a multitude of flavors, textures, colors, and heat. They range from the warm New Mexico, guajillo, and serrano to the mild California, ancho, Anaheim, pasilla, and Negro, to the hot cayenne, arbol, jalapeño, *pequin*, Japanese, Thai, bird, and tepin, to the hottest chile on earth, *habanero* (Scotch Bonnet). Tasting is recommended before adding to a dish. To do this, dip a toothpick in the seasoning and taste a minuscule amount to gauge how much heat to add. Following are the most common ways to keep chiles in the pantry. See also Hot Sauces (page 38), Chili Paste (page 20), and Chipotle Sauce (page 41).

Dried Whole Chiles. These must be soaked in boiling water to cover for 15 minutes or longer to soften before using. Varieties include crinkly pasilla, smooth red California, tiny pequin, maroon ancho, and pointy cayenne. After soaking, use large ones whole to make *chiles rellenos*, and the others chopped or pureed to add to sauces. Using a variety of chiles adds complex depth and aroma as well as heat.

Crushed Chiles. Often sold as crushed red pepper, these are dried and coarsely broken up, seeds and all, into flakes. Use them in stews or sauces, where they cook long enough to soften.

Ground Chiles. Cayenne pepper and other ground dried chiles such as *habanero* should be sautéed when using to get the full benefit of their impact. Add ground chiles to anything you want to have fire in it. Why not sprinkle some on bland bean dips or on a potato salad to get a hot bite here and there.

Chili Powder. See Blends and Rubs (page 29).

Canned Chiles. The small cans of green chiles use mild Anaheims, good for adding a little texture as well as a slightly sour dimension to soups and stews. Canned chipotles are very hot and should be used in moderation. See Chipotle Sauce (page 41).

COCONUT MILK

Always have a can or two on the shelf for Indonesian, Southeast Asian, and Caribbean dishes.

DRIED FRUIT

Raisins, prunes, apricots, and figs keep well for seasoning French pork sautés, Belgian rabbit or chicken stews, and Middle Eastern pilafs.

DRIED MUSHROOMS

Boletus (cèpes or porcini), morels, Chinese black (shiitake), and others keep well in a dry place. Add their earthy aromas and meaty textures to sauces, stews, and soups. I've also found dried mushroom powder and use it when I want to intensify the mushroom flavor of a pasta dish or sauce.

ENCHILADA SAUCE

Use like tomato sauce when you want spicy chile flavor.

FILÉ

This powder comes from the ground leaves of the native American sassafras tree. Its dusty green color and thickening power make it the signature ingredient along with okra in Creole gumbos. After adding filé to a dish, don't boil or it will become stringy.

FISH

Tuna or albacore and canned salmon add protein and flavor to Niçoise and Scandinavian potato salads and eclectic pasta sauces. Anchovies, too, are pizza-ready and an ingredient for salad dressing or Scandinavian potato dishes.

GINGER

See Pastes and Pestos, page 48.

NUTS

Keep sesame seeds for Chinese and African dishes, walnuts and almonds for Middle Eastern garnishes, pine nuts for Mediterranean food, and peanuts for West African and Southeast Asian fare. Dried unsweetened coconut for Indian curry sambals keeps well in the freezer, as do all the other nuts mentioned here. Peanut butter is a base for Indonesian peanut sauce.

OLIVES

Kalamata olives, green olives, Niçoise olives, and pimiento-stuffed olives lend the accents of the Mediterranean, Provence, and Spain to dishes they season. They also make quick appetizers.

PAPRIKA

Ground powder from the mild red chiles. Sprinkle on anything you are going to sauté, fry, or roast; it is a great browning agent.

PASTA

Pasta ingredients, shapes, and textures vary from Asia to the Mediterranean. Keep a variety of the following to add authenticity as well as surprise to your meals.

Asian Noodles. Rice noodles, egg noodles, bean threads, and rice sticks are all Asian staples. Noodles made from rice are thin and brittle and need only to be soaked to be rehydrated for soups or stir-fries. Bean threads, also known as cellophane or glass noodles, are made from ground mung beans. Soak them in warm water to rehydrate or fry them quickly in hot oil and see them expand to use as crisp additions to salads or "nests" for sauces.

Couscous. Morocco's pasta is made from durum wheat and processed into tiny kernels that cook in minutes.

Italian-style Noodles. Not just plain, these noodles are also flavored with garlic, beets, spinach, tomatoes, mushroom, chiles, and just about any herb or spice you can think of. Plain and flavored fettucine, linguine, and a limitless assortment of shapes (from grape bunches to chili peppers) are stocking the grocers' shelves. Dried, fresh, and frozen stuffed pasta such as ravioli, tortellini, and gnocchi are more options. Dried pasta will keep on the shelf for months. Fresh pasta must be refrigerated and used in a couple of days. Frozen keeps about six months. See Grains and Pasta (page 146) and Salads (page 106) for recipes.

Soba. Short fettucine-like noodles from Japan are made from buckwheat and are typically added to one of the cuisine's staples – dashi, a dried fish based broth. They are equally delicious in any other broth.

PEPPER

Green peppercorns are unripe berries with a tart, spicy taste and are usually packed in vinegar or water. They are especially good with meat sauces. Red or rose peppercorns are ripe and mild, and can be stirred whole into dishes or ground into a colorful sprinkle. Black peppercorns are dried berries and have the strongest bite. White peppercorns are also dried with the outer covering removed, which gives them less pungency. Use any of them whole for pickling and stocks, cracked for meats and salads, and ground for everything else.

PICKLES

Keep dill pickles on hand for tart-sour additions, and sweet pickles or relish for their sweet-tart hit. Pickled vegetables such as Italian giardiniera and other combinations can be stirred into salads and soups. Or put them on the table to perk up a bland stew or sauté.

POLENTA

America's indigenous grain, corn, found its way to Italy where, as a coarsely ground meal, it was embraced and glorified as a base as good as pasta for the sauces we think of as Italian. Easy to make (1 cup polenta is stirred into 4 cups boiling water and cooked until desired texture and consistency), it is also available premade and recipe ready, usually packaged in tube-shaped rolls. See recipe suggestions for Polenta (page 142).

PUMPKIN

Canned pumpkin in puree is great as a soup base or thickener.

REFRIED BEANS

Use to make burritos, thicken soups, or make into appetizer spreads with salsa, sour cream, and avocado.

RICE

The world's most popular grain comes in different types. See the recipes for Stove-top Rice (page 150) for cooking times.

Arborio Rice. Soft rice with a firm center, arborio comes from Italy, where it is the rice for risotto because it holds up well during the stove-top cooking.

Aromatic Rices. Grown in Asia and the United States, these fragrant grains are gaining popularity. Jasmine and basmati rice from Thailand and India have almost floral aromas and should be sauced with something light to maintain their aroma. American fragrant rices come from the South and are packaged as Texmati and Louisiana popcorn.

Black Rice. From Thailand and Vietnam, black rice is a dramatic addition to a plate of pastel ingredients.

Brown Rice. The whole kernel of the grain without the outer covering removed, which gives it a firm texture and nutty flavor. It requires longer cooking than white rice.

Converted Rice. On the fast cooking side, these grains have been steam-processed, which gives them a high nutritional factor and keeps them separate when cooking.

Instant Rice. Pre-cooked and dehydrated so that it can be cooked in about five minutes.

Long-grained White Rice. This all-purpose base for any sauce or seasoning possibility is the primary rice in Chinese and Indian dishes. I recommend rinsing it before cooking to keep the grains separated rather than gummy.

Short-grained White Rice. Typically used in Japanese cooking.

Sticky Rice. Also known as sweet rice, sticky rice is often used in Asian desserts. It is also used like bread in Thailand, formed into small balls to dip into sauces.

Wild Rice. This is not a real rice, but comes from a grass native to Minnesota. Its nutty flavor and distinctive chewy texture make it as usable as any true rice.

SAFFRON

The orange to dark yellow threads and powder impart a golden color and slightly musty flavor to rice and sauces for Indian dishes and Spanish paellas.

SESAME SEEDS

The delicious flavor of the tiny white or brown seeds has found a prominent place in sweet and savory cuisines of the Middle East, West Africa, China, Mexico, and South Carolina. Black sesame seeds are used in Asian dishes. For information on sesame oil, see page 23.

SPRAY OIL

Cans of olive and other oils with aerosol mechanisms are great for adding a little oil to a barbecue grill, for topping bread crumbs on baked tomatoes or eggplant, and for oiling pizza pans.

SUN-DRIED TOMATOES

Use these flavor-rich dried vegetables for pizza and pasta as well as for toppings for bread and ingredients for sauces. Choose those that are simply dried to stir into sauces and those packed in olive oil to use as a condiment for crostini or pizza.

SZECHUAN PEPPERCORNS

From a bush related to citrus, but not to black, rose, or white peppercorns, these peppercorns are ragged-shaped, reddish black, and intensely aromatic. Use these spicy additions in northern Chinese dishes and on any meat being readied for the grill. Also good in the stockpot.

TOMATOES

Whole and peeled, chopped, stewed, in puree or sauce, canned tomatoes are indispensable. Stir in some herb blends, a dollop of red pepper spread, and/or a favorite hot sauce and use them as soup or sauce bases for a world of flavors.

2

RECIPES

soups

Filling as an entrée or light and hunger-appeasing as a starter, **SOUP** is the most versatile of all the quick meal possibilities. A thick potato, a hearty vegetable, or a filling bean soup is a nutritious base that can be jazzed up to entertain the taste buds or kept pure as comfort food, depending on how it is seasoned. Stir in a spoonful or two of a favorite sauce, chutney, paste, or salsa for quick depth in a simple soup.

These soups can be made with homemade stock, canned broth, or water. Stock refers to unsalted homemade essences of meat, chicken, vegetables, or fish. Broth is usually salted, so be aware of the salt content when seasoning. Even more convenient are chicken, beef, fish and vegetable stock essences and concentrates. See Bouillon and Stock (page 34) for more information and Sources (page 248) for names of producers.

Vegetable Soup
page 72

Stock
page 68

Tomato Soup
page 74

RECIPE
LIST

Hot-and-Sour Soup
page 78

Legume Soup
page 80

Chowder
page 88

Potato Soup
page 84

Fish Soup
page 86

STOCK
makes about 1 gallon

Stocks are the backbone of good soups. Never add salt to the stockpot. A stock reduced to a syrupy glaze from meat is known as *glace de viande* and from chicken, *glace de poulet*. A fish stock is sometimes called *court bouillon*. Once the stock is made, strained, and cooled, it is easily frozen. Freezing it in ice cube trays and then putting the cubes in a freezer bag gives you a supply of convenient portions for deglazing a pan or braising vegetables.

1 to 2 onions, quartered

2 to 3 celery stalks with leaves, coarsely sliced

1 to 2 carrots, coarsely chopped

2 to 3 green onions or leeks, including green tops, chopped

1 bay leaf

Parsley sprigs

2 to 3 garlic cloves, smashed

6 black, white, or Szechuan peppercorns

1 tablespoon herb blend such as herbes de Provence, Italian blend, fines herbes, bouquet garni

5 quarts water

In a large, heavy stockpot, combine all the stock ingredients. Bring to a boil. With a slotted spoon, skim off any foam (to keep the stock clear). Reduce the heat to low, partly cover, and simmer as directed in the variations. Strain the stock and let it cool. Cover tightly and refrigerate for up to 5 days. Just before using, remove the fat that solidifies on top. To freeze, remove the fat and freeze the stock for up to 6 months.

VEGETABLE STOCK

Follow the master recipe, making these changes: Increase the vegetables by half again and add other vegetables without strong flavors such as tomatoes, mushrooms, squash, peppers. Also add an inch or so of peeled ginger or 1 teaspoon crushed or chopped ginger. Simmer 1 1/2 hours and finish as directed.

CHICKEN STOCK

To the master recipe, add 4 pounds chicken (or turkey) bones, especially legs and thighs, wing tips, necks and carcasses. (I save them in the freezer until I have enough to make stock.) Simmer 1 1/2 to 2 hours and finish as directed.

BEEF STOCK

To make a dark stock, combine the vegetables from the master recipe with 4 to 5 pounds beef (or pork or lamb) bones in a baking pan. (For a rich stock use leg or neck marrow bones.) Roast in an oven at 425 degrees F until browned, 45 to 60 minutes. Transfer them to a stockpot with the seasoning ingredients from the master recipe. Before adding the water, pour a cup or so of water into the hot roasting pan. Scrape the drippings from the bottom and pour into the stockpot. Alternatively, combine the meat bones in a stockpot with the other stock ingredients from the master recipe, cover with water by an inch or more. Simmer 3 to 4 hours and finish as directed.

FISH STOCK

To the master recipe, add 1 to 2 pounds fish carcasses, trim or bones, shrimp peelings, lobster or crab shells, or clam shells. (Add 1 to 2 teaspoons chopped peeled ginger if desired.) Continue as directed, cooking for 30 minutes.

GARLIC SOUP

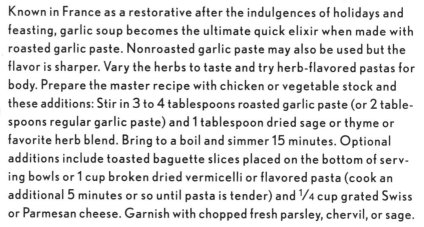

Known in France as a restorative after the indulgences of holidays and feasting, garlic soup becomes the ultimate quick elixir when made with roasted garlic paste. Nonroasted garlic paste may also be used but the flavor is sharper. Vary the herbs to taste and try herb-flavored pastas for body. Prepare the master recipe with chicken or vegetable stock and these additions: Stir in 3 to 4 tablespoons roasted garlic paste (or 2 tablespoons regular garlic paste) and 1 tablespoon dried sage or thyme or favorite herb blend. Bring to a boil and simmer 15 minutes. Optional additions include toasted baguette slices placed on the bottom of serving bowls or 1 cup broken dried vermicelli or flavored pasta (cook an additional 5 minutes or so until pasta is tender) and 1/4 cup grated Swiss or Parmesan cheese. Garnish with chopped fresh parsley, chervil, or sage.

MISO SOUP

Prepare the master recipe with vegetable or chicken stock and these additions: Stir in 1 carrot, sliced; 1/2 cup sliced mushrooms; and 2 green onions, including green tops, chopped. Bring to a boil, reduce heat to low, and simmer until carrots are tender, about 5 minutes. Mix a few tablespoons of the broth with 2 tablespoons of miso in a small bowl and pour it into the soup. Stir and keep warm. Optional additions include 4 ounces cubed soft or firm tofu, 1/2 cup bean sprouts or bamboo shoots, or 1/2 cup broken dried soba (buckwheat) noodles or other dried noodles. Add noodles and cook until tender before stirring in the miso, as the miso should not boil.

VIETNAMESE NOODLE SOUP

Prepare the master recipe with beef stock and these additions: 1 teaspoon minced peeled ginger, 1 star anise (optional), 2 tablespoons fish sauce (*nuoc mam*), and the juice of 1 lime. Bring to a boil. Stir in 4 ounces dried vermicelli or 2 ounces fresh Asian egg noodles and cook until tender, about 5 minutes. Thinly slice across the grain 1/4 pound top round or sirloin. Drop the slices into the boiling soup along with 1 cup bean sprouts and 2 green onions, including green tops, chopped. The beef will take 2 to 3 minutes to cook. Add salt and freshly ground black pepper to taste. Garnish the soup with chopped fresh cilantro and chile paste with garlic.

EGG DROP SOUP

Prepare the master recipe with chicken or vegetable stock. Bring to a boil, stir in 1/3 cup raw rice, and cook until rice is tender, 8 to 15 minutes. In a mixing bowl, beat 2 or 3 eggs until light and frothy. Ladle some of the hot stock into the eggs, whisking constantly. Add about half of the stock, and continue whisking, then pour the egg mixture into the soup pot. Reduce the heat to low, and continue whisking to incorporate the egg, not curdle it. For Chinese egg drop, stir in 2 teaspoons soy sauce (or to taste) and garnish with chopped fresh parsley. Add salt and freshly ground black pepper to taste. For Greek avgolemono, after rice is tender lower the heat until the liquid no longer boils. Stir in the eggs, then the juice of 2 lemons. Garnish with chopped fresh parsley or snipped fresh chives.

WONTON SOUP

Prepare the master recipe with chicken or vegetable stock and these additions: Stir in 1 teaspoon chopped peeled ginger; 3 green onions, including green tops, chopped; 1 to 2 tablespoons soy sauce; 1/4 to 1/2 teaspoon chile paste with garlic, and a drop of roasted sesame oil. Bring the soup to a boil. Drop in 12 frozen or fresh wontons, lower heat, and simmer until wontons are cooked through, 5 to 10 minutes. Garnish with chopped fresh parsley or green onions.

PASTA AND BEAN SOUP

Prepare the master recipe with chicken or vegetable stock and these additions: Stir in 1 to 2 teaspoons garlic paste and 1 tablespoon Italian herb blend and bring to a boil. Add 1 cup of small shaped dried pasta or spaghetti broken into 1-inch pieces, and cook until tender, about 10 minutes. Stir in 1 1/2 cups (or one 15-ounce can, drained and rinsed) cooked white, red, or garbanzo beans and 2 Roma tomatoes, chopped. Add salt and freshly ground black pepper to taste. Simmer for 5 to 10 minutes to blend flavors. Stir in 1/2 cup chopped fresh parsley.

BROTH WITH STUFFED PASTA

Prepare the master recipe with chicken or vegetable stock and these additions: Stir in 1 cup tomato pasta sauce and 1 teaspoon garlic paste. Bring to a boil. Stir in 1 pound fresh or frozen tortellini and cook until pasta is tender, 5 to 10 minutes. Add salt and freshly ground black pepper to taste. Garnish with chopped fresh basil or parsley.

VEGETABLE SOUP

serves 6 to 8

Combinations of cooked and fresh vegetables can be included, but put in the fresh ones before adding those already cooked. While specific amounts of vegetables are given, it's fine to add more or less according to your taste. This soup also puts leftover pasta sauces or vegetable relishes to good use.

10 to 12 cups vegetable, chicken, or beef stock; canned broth; or water

6 cups chopped raw or cooked vegetables such as onions, leeks, carrots, celery, potatoes, green beans, spinach, zucchini, or yellow squash

2 garlic cloves, minced

1 tablespoon any herb blend

Salt and freshly ground black pepper

1 cup cooked beans (optional)

Pour the stock into a 6-quart soup pot. Add the uncooked vegetables first, then stir in the garlic, herbs, and salt and pepper to taste. Bring to a boil and simmer until vegetables are tender. Then stir in the cooked vegetables and beans (if using) and heat to serving temperature.

PROVENÇAL PISTOU

For the beloved *soupe au pistou* of the south of France, prepare the master recipe and pass pesto at the table to stir into the finished soup. Heat the pesto if frozen or ladle it straight from the jar.

INDIAN CURRY SOUP

You can use curry powder or paste. For paste, add 2 to 4 tablespoons to the stock with the other seasonings. With curry powder, rearrange the master recipe as follows: In the soup pot, warm 2 tablespoons vegetable oil over medium heat and stir in the onions (and onion relatives). When they are softened, stir in 2 to 3 tablespoons curry powder and the garlic. Sauté about 30 seconds to bring up the oils in the spices. Then add the rest of the vegetables, the herbs, and stock. Bring to a boil, reduce heat to medium, and cook until everything is tender, 20 to 30 minutes. Stir in 1 cup of peas (fresh, or defrosted if frozen) before serving, if you like. Or stir in a few tablespoons of chutney and a spoonful of plain yogurt.

MEXICAN TORTILLA SOUP

Prepare the master recipe with these changes: When the vegetables are tender, stir in 2 tablespoons mole paste, 1/2 to 3/4 cup salsa, and 1 1/2 cups (or one 15-ounce can, drained and rinsed) cooked black or red beans. Tear 2 corn tortillas into bite-sized pieces and add to the soup (they will soften and dissolve slightly to thicken the soup). Garnish with chopped fresh cilantro.

ITALIAN MINESTRONE

Prepare the master recipe using Italian herb blend. When the vegetables are tender, stir in 1 cup or more caponata or other Mediterranean vegetable relish; 1 cup tomato sauce or pasta sauce; and 1 1/2 cups cooked (or one 15-ounce can, drained and rinsed) white, kidney, or lima beans. After simmering for about 15 minutes, stir in a small dried pasta such as melone and cook until tender, about 10 minutes longer. Garnish with grated Parmesan cheese and plenty of chopped fresh basil.

CARIBBEAN PEPPERPOT

Prepare the master recipe with these additions: After adding the stock, stir in a teaspoon or so of a Caribbean hot sauce – be careful with amounts since these sauces contain the fiery *habanero* chile. Add a few handfuls of chopped fresh kale, spinach, or collard greens and cook until tender. Alternatively, substitute a teaspoon or so of jerk seasoning for the Caribbean hot sauce. Garnish with fresh lime wedges.

TOMATO SOUP

serves 3 to 4

Everybody's favorite soup has to be the easiest to make, winter or summer. When fresh tomatoes aren't available, canned ones are fine substitutes because they are processed at the peak of the season, ensuring a ripe, red base for soup. Other pantry items include tomato pasta sauces for the base and additions of pesto, tapenade, salsa, nut butters, and chutneys. For more concentrated tomato taste, stir in a few ounces of chopped sun-dried tomatoes or a dried tomato seasoning.

2 tablespoons vegetable or olive oil

1 onion, chopped

2 garlic cloves, chopped, or 1 teaspoon garlic paste

4 cups chopped fresh tomatoes or one 28-ounce can chopped or crushed tomatoes

6 cups chicken or vegetable stock, canned broth, or water

Salt and freshly ground black or white pepper

Garnishes: fresh parsley, plain yogurt or sour cream, chutney, fresh goat cheese

In a soup pot over medium heat, warm the oil. Sauté the onion until soft, about 3 minutes. Stir in the garlic and cook about 15 seconds more. Stir in the tomatoes and stock. Bring the soup to a boil, reduce heat, and simmer 15 minutes. If you want a smooth texture, transfer the soup solids with a slotted spoon to a blender or food processor and puree. Return to the soup pot and heat to serving temperature. Season with salt and pepper to taste. Garnish with a sprinkling of parsley, a spoonful of plain yogurt or chutney, or a small piece of goat cheese.

SPICY TOMATO SOUP

Prepare the master recipe, following either of these variations: When sautéing the chopped onion, just after it is soft add 1 minced fresh or canned chile, or 1 teaspoon cayenne pepper, or a pinch of ground *habanero* (the hottest chile on earth!), or $1/2$ teaspoon crushed red pepper. Alternatively, when you add the tomatoes, stir in $1/4$ teaspoon (or to taste) of chile paste or cayenne pepper. Serve the soup with dollops of cooling plain yogurt or a few ounces of goat cheese.

SWEET AND GARLICKY TOMATO SOUP

Prepare the master recipe with these changes: Use roasted-garlic olive oil. Instead of the fresh garlic, use 2 teaspoons roasted garlic paste. Grate 1 or 2 carrots and sauté with the onion. Garnish with chopped fresh parsley or snipped fresh chives.

MEXICAN TOMATO SOUP

Prepare the master recipe with these additions: Sauté $1/2$ green bell pepper, seeded and chopped, with the onion. With the garlic, stir in 2 to 3 teaspoons of Mexican herb blend or chili powder and cook about 30 seconds. Puree, if you like. Optional additions include 1 cup cooked rice or corn kernels; 1 corn tortilla, torn into bite-sized pieces; $1/2$ cup salsa; dried tomato seasoning; or a Mexican sauce; plus chopped fresh cilantro for garnish.

AFRICAN PEANUT TOMATO SOUP

Prepare the master recipe with these additions: Sauté $1/2$ red bell pepper, seeded and chopped, with the onion. With the garlic, add a pinch of ground *habanero* (hot!). After the stock is added and comes to a boil, stir in $1/3$ cup raw white or brown rice (or $3/4$ cup cooked). Cook until rice is tender, 15 to 20 minutes. Ladle $1/3$ cup hot soup into a bowl over $1/2$ cup creamy peanut butter and stir to blend. Then, pour this mixture into the soup. Bring to serving temperature and serve with chopped roasted peanuts and chopped fresh cilantro or parsley.

HUNGARIAN TOMATO SOUP

Prepare the master recipe with these changes: Sauté 1 pimiento, finely chopped, or $1/2$ red bell pepper, seeded and finely chopped, with the onion. With the garlic, stir in $1\frac{1}{2}$ teaspoons paprika. With the tomatoes, add 1 to 2 ounces bacon, chopped, cooked crisp, and drained, or 1 to 2 ounces chopped ham. Don't puree the soup. Cook as directed. Garnish with dollops of sour cream or plain yogurt and snipped fresh chives.

GAZPACHO

For this cold, uncooked soup, use fresh tomatoes and all the ingredients in the master recipe except the oil. Use 2 to 3 cups of stock. Combine them in a bowl and add the following: $1/2$ cucumber, peeled and finely chopped; 2 green onions, including green tops, chopped; 1 green bell pepper, seeded and finely chopped; 1 to 2 tablespoons wine vinegar or lemon juice; 2 teaspoons of a favorite herb blend or $1/4$ to $1/2$ teaspoon each of dried oregano, dried basil, dried marjoram, and ground cumin; cayenne pepper to taste; and $1/2$ cup finely chopped fresh parsley.

PANTRY
TIPS

Clean out the refrigerator! Soups are the perfect use for odds and ends of red pepper spreads, chutneys, pasta sauces, and relishes.

Canned pumpkin is an effective thickener for a thin soup that also adds a distinctive flavor.

Add 1 cup cooked rice to 6 or 8 cups of soup just before serving. Or, to use the starch from rice as a thickener, stir in $1/3$ cup raw rice when the soup is boiling, and cook until the rice is tender, about 15 minutes.

HOT-AND-SOUR SOUP

serves 4 to 6

Asian food markets stock bases for hot-and-sour soups in jars. Finding one you like that is not too salty, too hot, or too sour is a matter of experimentation. Here is a master recipe for that special flavor followed by variations that give the soup a Thai or Chinese accent.

6 cups chicken stock or canned broth

2 to 3 dried black mushrooms, soaked in hot water for 15 minutes, then sliced into julienne strips

1 tablespoon finely chopped peeled ginger

4 green onions, including green tops, finely chopped

1 garlic clove, minced, or $1/2$ teaspoon garlic paste

$1/4$ to $1/2$ teaspoon chile paste with garlic

Juice of 2 limes

2 tablespoons soy sauce

Chopped green onions or fresh parsley, for garnish

In a soup pot, combine the stock with all of the ingredients except the garnish. Bring to a boil, then reduce the heat and simmer 5 minutes or so to blend the flavors. Garnish and serve.

THAI HOT-AND-SOUR SOUP

Prepare the master recipe with these changes: Add 1 to 2 tablespoons Thai seasoning or Thai curry mix seasoning; substitute 2 tablespoons fish sauce for the soy sauce. Simmer for 15 to 20 minutes. Add seafood (see Hot-and-Sour Seafood Soup, below) if you like. Serve garnished with chopped fresh cilantro or parsley.

CHINESE HOT-AND-SOUR SOUP

Prepare the master recipe with these changes: Add $1/8$ to $1/4$ teaspoon ground Szechuan peppercorns; substitute 1 tablespoon miso for the soy sauce. Optional additions include 4 ounces firm or soft tofu, cubed; $1/2$ cup bamboo shoots, chopped; and a half ounce or so of dried tree ears or tiger lily buds.

JAPANESE MISO HOT-AND-SOUR SOUP

Prepare the master recipe substituting 1 tablespoon (or to taste) of any miso for the soy sauce. Add 2 to 3 ounces of dried soba (buckwheat) noodles and cook until tender, about 8 minutes. Garnish with snipped fresh chives.

HOT-AND-SOUR SEAFOOD SOUP

Prepare the master recipe as directed. About 5 minutes before serving add $1/2$ pound medium shrimp, shelled and deveined, and $1/2$ pound of scallops. Cook over medium heat until shellfish is cooked through, about 5 minutes. Garnish with chopped fresh cilantro and lime wedges.

LEGUME SOUP

serves 4 to 6

Be sure all the beans are tender before adding any acidic ingredients such as tomatoes, which inhibit their cooking.

3 cups cooked legumes ($1/2$ pound dried) or two 15-ounce cans beans, drained and rinsed

1 teaspoon salt or 1 to 2 ounces blanched bacon or a ham hock

8 cups water, vegetable or chicken stock, or canned broth

2 tablespoons canola or safflower oil

2 onions, chopped

2 celery stalks, chopped

2 carrots, chopped

3 garlic cloves, minced, or $1\,1/2$ teaspoons garlic paste

1 tablespoon herb blend

Salt and freshly ground black or white pepper

Garnishes: chopped fresh parsley or cilantro, grated cheese, snipped fresh chives, chutney, salsa or hot sauce

If using dried beans, soak and cook them as directed on page 126. In a large soup pot, warm the oil over medium-high heat and sauté the onions, celery, and carrots until softened, about 5 minutes. Stir in the garlic and sauté another 30 seconds. Add the herbs, then stir in the cooked beans, salt, and water, stock, or broth. Bring to a boil, reduce the heat, and simmer until the flavors have blended, 15 to 20 minutes. Either puree the beans in a blender or food processor or leave them whole. If they're pureed, you may need to add more liquid to make it soupy. Season to taste with salt and pepper and garnish of choice.

SOUTHWESTERN BEAN SOUP

Prepare the master recipe using black or red beans and these changes: Use a Mexican or Southwestern herb blend and add 1 cup tomato sauce and 1 cup salsa when you stir in the beans and liquid. Simmer for 15 to 20 minutes. Don't puree. Garnish with chopped fresh cilantro, chopped fresh tomatoes, cubed avocado drizzled with fresh lime juice, and grated Monterey jack or Cheddar cheese.

MIDDLE EASTERN LENTIL SOUP

Prepare the master recipe using cooked lentils (they take 25 to 30 minutes to cook). Sauté the vegetables and garlic as directed. Use a Middle Eastern herb blend or a bean herb blend and add 14 ounces chopped canned tomatoes with their juice. Stir in 2 to 4 tablespoons harissa and the juice of 1/2 lemon. Simmer 15 to 20 minutes. Garnish with red pepper spread or more harissa.

BRAZILIAN BLACK BEAN SOUP

This is a soupy version of *feijoada*, the national dish of Brazil. Prepare the master recipe using black beans and add a ham hock when cooking the beans. When the beans are tender, puree if you like. Remove the meat from the ham hock bone, cut it up finely, and stir it back into the beans. Sauté the vegetables and garlic as directed in the master recipe. For the herbs, use a bean herb blend or a combination of dried oregano, basil, and parsley. Add more liquid if necessary to make it soupy. Simmer beans as directed for 15 minutes. Meanwhile, sauté 1/2 pound chorizo and add it to the beans. Simmer another 10 minutes. Garnish with chopped fresh cilantro, lime wedges, and hot sauce.

CREOLE RED BEAN SOUP

Prepare the master recipe using red beans with these changes: Sauté 1 green bell pepper, seeded and chopped, with the other vegetables. For the herbs, use a Creole or Cajun herb blend. Season to taste with Tabasco or other Louisiana hot sauce. Don't puree the soup. Optional additions include hot link sausages, sliced and sautéed, or shelled and cooked crawfish. Garnish with chopped fresh parsley and pass more hot sauce.

FRENCH WHITE BEAN SOUP

Prepare the master recipe using French flageolet cannellini, or Great Northern beans. For the herbs, use a dry blend, either fines herbes or herbes de Provence. About 5 minutes before serving, add 1/2 teaspoon garlic paste to bring up the garlic flavor. Garnish with plenty of chopped fresh parsley (green herbs help keep away garlic breath!).

SPLIT PEA SOUP

Prepare the master recipe using yellow or green split peas and with these changes: Cook the peas with a ham hock, if you like. Cut the meat, if using, off the bone and stir into the soup. For the herbs, use any favorite herb blend. When the peas are tender, either puree them in a blender or food processor or leave as is for more texture. Optional additions include 1 or 2 carrots, grated and sautéed with the onions or 2 to 3 ounces chopped ham added just before serving. Garnish with a bit of fresh goat cheese or a spiral of red pepper spread.

PANTRY
TIPS

Ramen noodles without their seasoning packets add fast-cooking substance to homemade broths and tomato soups.

Refried beans are excellent as a soup base: Thin with stock, broth, or water and add leftover cooked vegetables, a can of tomatoes or tomato sauce, and plenty of herbs and garlic.

POTATO SOUP

serves 4 to 6

Coming from an Irish-American family, I can't think of a more comfortable ingredient than potatoes. The master recipe reflects the soothing, feel-good characteristics of potatoes and the variations show how they can back up the most brazen spices. Red and white rose potatoes are firm and give a slightly glossy finish to a pureed potato soup. Russets, which are more starchy, end up with a hearty opaque texture. Peel the potatoes if you like, but their finely minced skins make a nice addition to the soup. Always use a food mill or a potato masher to puree potatoes. A blender or food processor will make potatoes gummy.

2 tablespoons canola or safflower oil or butter

1 onion, chopped

1 to 2 leeks, white part only, chopped (optional)

2 garlic cloves, or 1 teaspoon garlic paste

6 medium potatoes (about 3 pounds), peeled or unpeeled and cubed (about 6 cups)

1 to 2 carrots, grated (optional)

6 cups chicken or vegetable stock, canned broth, or water

Salt and freshly ground black or white pepper

1 cup milk or cream (optional)

Chopped fresh parsley or snipped fresh chives, for garnish

In a large soup pot over medium heat, warm the oil. Sauté the onion, leeks (if using), garlic, potatoes, and carrots (if using) for 3 to 4 minutes. When the onions have softened, stir in the stock, raise the heat, and bring to a boil. Lower the heat to medium and cook until the potatoes are tender, about 15 minutes. If you don't want a pureed soup, add the milk or cream and heat to serving temperature. For a pureed soup, using a large slotted spoon, transfer the potatoes to a food mill or mash them with a potato masher or a fork. Puree until smooth. Return the puree to the soup pot. Season to taste with salt and pepper. Stir in the milk or cream and heat to serving temperature. Garnish with chopped fresh parsley or snipped fresh chives.

COLOMBIAN AJIACO

Prepare the master recipe with these changes: For the potatoes, use a combination of russets, white rose, and sweet potatoes or yams. Substitute 6 green onions for the leeks. Add 2 to 3 tablespoons Mexican or South American herb blend, and 1/4 cup chopped fresh cilantro when you add the stock. When the potatoes are tender, stir in 1 1/2 cups corn kernels and cook a minute longer. Taste for seasoning. Garnish with hot sauce, chopped avocado sprinkled with fresh lime juice, and chopped fresh cilantro.

CREAMY GARLIC POTATO SOUP

Prepare the master as directed, but increase the garlic to 5 cloves or use 1 1/2 tablespoons garlic paste or 2 tablespoons roasted garlic paste.

INDIAN CURRIED POTATO SOUP

Prepare the master recipe with these changes: Sauté 2 to 3 tablespoons curry powder with the onion. If using curry paste add it with the stock. When the potatoes are tender, don't puree. Stir in 1 cup peas with the milk and cook until heated through. Garnish with chopped fresh parsley and a spoonful of chutney, plain yogurt, or sambal if desired.

CARIBBEAN POTATO SOUP

Prepare the master recipe using half russet and half sweet potatoes or yams. Sauté the onion with 1 teaspoon jerk seasoning or Caribbean hot sauce. When the potatoes are tender, stir in 2 cups chopped fresh spinach (or one 10-ounce package frozen chopped spinach, thawed) kale, or collard greens and cook until tender – 1 minute for spinach, 6 to 8 minutes for kale, and 10 to 15 minutes for collards. Substitute 1 cup coconut milk for the milk, if you like, then heat to serving temperature.

GERMAN POTATO SOUP

Prepare the master recipe with these changes: For 2 of the potatoes, substitute one turnip, peeled and cubed; 1 rutabaga, peeled and cubed; and 1 carrot, grated. When the vegetables are tender, stir in 2 cups rinsed sauerkraut. Don't puree, and leave out the milk. Heat to serving temperature. Garnish with a dollop of sour cream, a sprinkling of paprika, and snipped fresh chives.

FISH SOUP

serves 4

I live close to the Pacific Ocean, so fresh fish is always available. As a habit, I often lean toward Mediterranean seasonings and herbs when I make soups. When they aren't the taste I crave, it's great to know I can change the taste to reflect the sunny coastlines of the Caribbean, Mexico, and Thailand just by opening a jar or bottle of seasonings. It's always a one-pot, no-fuss meal.

2 tablespoons canola, safflower, or olive oil

1/2 onion, finely chopped

1/2 red or green bell pepper, seeded and chopped (optional)

2 garlic cloves, minced, or 1 teaspoon garlic paste

6 cups fish or vegetable stock, canned broth, or water

1 to 2 tablespoons dried herbs or herb blend

1 to 11/2 pounds fish fillets and/or shellfish, cut into bite-sized pieces

Salt and freshly ground black or white pepper

Chopped fresh parsley and/or snipped fresh chives, for garnish

In a soup pot, warm the oil over medium heat. Sauté the onion and bell pepper until softened, 2 to 3 minutes. Add the garlic and sauté another 30 seconds. Stir in the stock and herbs and bring to a boil. Reduce heat to medium and simmer 15 minutes to blend flavors. Drop the fish into the soup and simmer until the fish is firm and just cooked, 3 to 5 minutes. Season to taste with salt and pepper. Garnish with parsley and/or chives.

CARIBBEAN CRAB SOUP

Prepare the master recipe with these changes: As the onion and bell pepper sauté, stir in 1 teaspoon (or to taste) Caribbean hot sauce. Substitute 1 1/2 cups coconut milk for 2 cups of the stock. After the stock has simmered, stir in 4 to 5 ounces crabmeat instead of the fish. Season to taste and heat to serving temperature. Garnish with chopped fresh cilantro and lime wedges. Pass more Caribbean hot sauce to taste.

PROVENÇAL BOURRIDE

Prepare the master recipe with these changes: For the herbs, use herbes de Provence, fines herbes, or a combination of dried basil and marjoram. Substitute one 12-ounce can (1 1/2 cups) stewed tomatoes or crushed tomatoes in puree for 2 cups of the stock. When the soup is finished, garnish with a rouille made from 1/3 cup red pepper spread mixed with 1/2 to 1 teaspoon garlic paste, a dash of cayenne pepper, and chopped fresh basil.

MEDITERRANEAN MUSSEL SOUP

Prepare the master recipe omitting the green bell pepper and with these changes: Substitute 1 1/2 cups marinara or other pasta sauce and 1 cup dry white wine for 4 cups of the stock. Use Italian herb blend. After the sauce has simmered for 15 minutes, stir in 4 to 5 pounds steamed mussels in their shells instead of the fish. Garnish with chopped fresh parsley or basil.

CREOLE FISH SOUP

Prepare the master recipe using a green bell pepper and these changes: Add 1/2 red bell pepper, seeded and chopped, and 1 or 2 celery stalks, chopped, to the vegetables if desired. Substitute 8 ounces tomato sauce or Creole sauce for 1 cup of the stock or water. Use Creole or Cajun herb blend. For the fish, use 1 to 2 pounds of crawfish tails only, or a combination of crawfish tails, peeled and deveined shrimp, and rockfish fillets, cut into bite-sized pieces.

PORTUGUESE FISHERMAN'S SOUP

Begin the master recipe and use a green bell pepper. When the vegetables are soft, add 1 or 2 sliced new or russet potatoes and the liquid, but substitute 1 cup dry white wine for 1 cup of the stock. Stir in 6 ounces tomato paste. Cook until the potatoes are tender, then drop in 1 pound scrubbed mussels; 1/4 pound medium shrimp, shelled and deveined; and 4 to 6 ounces fish fillets, cut into bite-sized pieces. Garnish with chopped fresh cilantro and garlic toast.

CHOWDER

serves 4

Like potato soup, a chowder has a homey appeal. It needn't be limited to clams when there is corn and salmon available and a whole pantry of seasonal embellishments to transform it into something new. This one starts with a roux that helps with thickening so you don't have to depend on a lot of cream. If you like, substitute flavored oils for the vegetable oil, and add herb blends to the master recipe.

3 tablespoons canola or safflower oil

2 tablespoons all-purpose flour

1/2 to 1 onion, chopped

1 to 2 celery stalks, chopped

1 garlic clove, chopped, or 1/2 teaspoon garlic paste

2 potatoes, peeled or unpeeled and cubed

6 cups chicken or vegetable stock, canned broth, or water

1/2 to 1 cup milk, half and half, or cream

Salt and ground white or black **pepper**

Chopped fresh parsley, for garnish

In a soup pot over medium heat, warm the oil. Add the flour and cook, stirring constantly, until the flour is just beginning to turn color, 1 to 3 minutes. Stir in the onion and celery and sauté 2 to 3 minutes to soften. Add the garlic and potatoes and sauté about 30 seconds more. Slowly pour in the stock, stirring all the while. Bring to a boil, then reduce heat to medium and cook until the potatoes are tender, 6 to 10 minutes. Add the milk and heat to serving temperature. Add salt and pepper to taste. Serve hot, garnished with chopped parsley.

CLAM CHOWDER

Prepare the master recipe with these changes: Substitute 1 cup clam juice for 1 cup stock. Stir in 2 to 3 pounds fresh clams just after the potatoes are tender and before the milk is added. If using canned clams, stir in with the milk.

CORN CHOWDER

Prepare the master recipe with these changes: When adding the flour also stir in 2 teaspoons Mexican or Southwestern herb blend. When adding the onion, also add 1/2 red bell pepper, seeded and chopped, and 1/2 green bell pepper, seeded and chopped. When the potatoes are tender, puree them in a food mill or mash them with a fork, if you like, and return the mixture to the pot. Stir in 3 cups corn kernels. Then add the milk and heat to serving temperature. Garnish with chopped fresh cilantro and avocado cubes that have been drizzled with fresh lime or lemon juice.

CARIBBEAN CHOWDER

Prepare the master recipe with these changes: When adding the onions, also add 1/2 green bell pepper, seeded and chopped, and 3 green onions, chopped, including green tops. With the stock stir in a teaspoon or so of Caribbean hot sauce (to taste). After the potatoes have cooked, stir in 3/4 pound medium shrimp, shelled and deveined. Substitute coconut milk for the milk and heat to serving temperature. Garnish with chopped fresh cilantro and cubes of mango if desired. Pass around more Caribbean hot sauce.

TOMATO CHOWDER

Prepare the master recipe with these changes: Sauté 1/2 red bell pepper, seeded and chopped, with the onion and celery. Substitute 3 cups chopped tomatoes, crushed tomatoes in puree, or chunky tomato pasta sauce for 3 cups of the stock. Omit the potatoes. Just before serving, stir in 1/2 cup cream and heat to serving temperature. Garnish with red pepper spread and chopped fresh basil or parsley.

Stocking your pantry with a variety of herbs, sauces, and seasonings means quick, convenient **SALADS.** I like to add a drop of sesame oil to a dressing for a green or rice salad, a few spoonfuls of pesto to a pasta salad, a tablespoon or two of curry paste to a potato salad, and always a different kind of mustard to a vinaigrette. Here are some other ways I've found to jazz up a salad from the pantry.

Slaw

page 96

Rice Salad

page 98

**Classic
Potato Salad**

page 102

Salad Dressing

page 94

RECIPE
LIST

**Sliced and Cooked
Potato Salad**

page 104

Pasta Salad

page 106

Bean Salad

page 110

SALAD DRESSING

makes about ¹/₂ cup

I keep a selection of oils, vinegars, and mustards on hand to mix into a quick dressing, or make a triple or quadruple batch to use over several days. The flavor varies each time depending on the combination, and the dressing always tastes fresh. Hazelnut oil on a salad with avocado or blanched green vegetables creates an incredible match of flavors. Seasoned rice vinegar adds a bit of sweetness and raspberry vinegar a fruitiness, both refreshing finishes for an after-entrée salad.

Store specialty and flavored oils in the refrigerator. No oil should be stored at temperatures over 70 degrees F. In general, monounsaturated oils such as olive oil keep better than polyunsaturated. Unrefined oils keep better than refined, which have their natural antioxidants processed out. The most stable oils are safflower, canola, corn, peanut, and sesame. If an oil solidifies, it will return to liquid state when brought to room temperature. You have several options for the garlic addition. Minced fresh garlic gives the strongest flavor. Putting a clove on a toothpick imparts a mellowerflavor that intensifies the longer you leave it in the dressing. Crushed garlic has a stronger flavor, while roasted garlic paste is slightly sweet.

2 to 4 tablespoons flavored vinegar such as wine, cider, rice, garlic, herb, or berry

¹/₂ cup safflower, canola, olive, or flavored oil

1 garlic clove, minced, or 1 whole clove skewered on a toothpick, or ¹/₄ to ¹/₂ teaspoon garlic paste or roasted garlic paste

Salt and freshly ground black or white pepper

Combine all the ingredients in a jar with a tight-fitting lid and shake to blend.

ASIAN DRESSING

Prepare the master recipe using 2 tablespoons rice vinegar, $1/4$ teaspoon toasted sesame oil, and 6 tablespoons canola or safflower oil.

MUSTARD DRESSING

Prepare the master dressing and add $1/2$ teaspoon dry mustard or 2 to 3 teaspoons or more of any prepared mustard. Enhance the flavor of the mustard by adding complementary ingredients in the salad, such as orange sections with an orange-flavored mustard.

ITALIAN DRESSING

Prepare the master dressing with olive oil and red wine vinegar and stir in 1 tablespoon Italian herb blend.

CREAMY RANCH DRESSING

Prepare the master recipe and substitute $1/4$ cup regular or garlic-flavored mayonnaise for half of the oil.

FRENCH DRESSING

Prepare the master dressing using white wine vinegar and olive oil and add 1 teaspoon Dijon-style mustard.

RASPBERRY DRESSING

Prepare the master dressing with raspberry vinegar and olive oil and add $1/4$ to $1/2$ teaspoon dry or prepared mustard.

GINGER DRESSING

Prepare the master dressing with ginger-flavored oil or vinegar. Add peeled grated ginger or chopped ginger from a jar to intensify the flavor. Use in potato or pasta salads as well as with mixed greens.

DIJON-STYLE DRESSING

A friend in New York with French heritage inspired this classic dressing. Prepare the master recipe using $1/4$ cup Dijon-style mustard, 1 tablespoon red wine vinegar, $1 1/2$ tablespoons olive oil, 1 garlic clove, minced, and salt and freshly ground black pepper. It is very thick and wonderful spread on vine-ripened tomato slices. (My friend also adds sautéed scallops to the mustard-covered tomatoes.)

S LAW

serves 8 to 10

Sweet or sour, with a pickle or a pepper, cole or cabbage slaws reflect the taste of the makers. Here is a basic recipe, one of the quickest of all recipes, plus a few suggestions to create the taste you like. Garlic, cumin, and lemon-flavored mayonnaise or infused oils and vinegars are also options to personalize the flavors here. One of my favorite slaws is shredded cabbage simply dressed with tarragon vinegar and roasted garlic mayonnaise.

1 small head green or red cabbage, shredded (about 8 cups)

$^1/_2$ cup plain or flavored mayonnaise

$^1/_4$ cup safflower or canola oil

2 to 4 tablespoons vinegar

2 teaspoons hot-sweet, coarse grain, or other mustard

1 garlic clove, minced, or $^1/_2$ teaspoon garlic paste

1 carrot, grated, or 1 red bell pepper, seeded and chopped (optional)

Salt and freshly ground black or white pepper

Place the cabbage in a large mixing bowl. In a small bowl, combine the mayonnaise, oil, vinegar, mustard, garlic, and carrot or bell pepper (if using), and salt and pepper to taste; pour over the cabbage. Let stand at least 30 minutes for flavors to blend before serving.

SWEET-SOUR SLAW

Prepare the master recipe with these changes: Substitute 1/2 cup sweet-and-sour sauce for the mayonnaise and stir in 1/2 green bell pepper, seeded and chopped. Additionally, add 1/2 to 1 cup cubed fresh or canned pineapple, if you like.

SOUTHERN SWEET SLAW

Prepare the master recipe and add 3 to 5 tablespoons pickle relish.

MUSTARD SLAW

For a tart yellow slaw, prepare the master recipe with these changes: Add 2 to 4 tablespoons yellow mustard. For another aromatic and textured taste add a whole grain mustard, a red pepper mustard, or an orange-chile mustard.

SESAME SLAW

Prepare the master recipe with these changes: Substitute 2 teaspoons toasted sesame oil for half of the vegetable oil. Add 1/2 red bell pepper, seeded and chopped, and 1 carrot, grated. Sprinkle with a teaspoon or so of toasted sesame seeds.

HOT SLAW

Prepare the cabbage and carrot as directed in the master recipe. Add 1/2 onion, chopped, and 1 green bell pepper, seeded and chopped. For the dressing, omit the mayonnaise and prepare as follows: Combine 1/3 cup pepper-garlic vinegar, 1/3 cup canola or safflower oil, and 2 tablespoons sugar in a saucepan and bring to a boil. Pour the hot dressing over the cabbage mixture and stir well. Season with salt and pepper to taste. Serve at room temperature.

KIM CHEE

Prepare the cabbage, carrots, and 1 red bell pepper as directed in the master recipe. For the dressing, substitute the following: Heat 1 to 4 tablespoons of kim chee base (to taste), thinned with 1/2 cup water or stock just to boiling. Pour the hot dressing over the cabbage mixture and stir well. Serve at room temperature.

RICE SALAD
serves 4

Rice salad is such a favorite in my house, I cook extra rice for dinner to have enough for the next day's lunch. Dressings from a bottle or a combination of flavored oils and vinegars give a different taste every time I make one. So do a variety of additions such as ham, chicken, sausage, red bell peppers, chopped fresh basil, and — my favorite — chopped apple. Pantry ingredients to add include chutneys, flavored mayonnaise, caponata, pickled vegetables, relishes, artichoke hearts, mustard, capers, and olives. For how to cook rice, see page 150.

$1/3$ to $1/2$ cup olive oil

2 to 4 tablespoons vinegar

1 tablespoon mustard (optional)

1 to 2 garlic cloves, minced, or $1/2$ to 1 teaspoon garlic paste

Salt and freshly ground black or white pepper

4 cups cooked white, brown, or wild rice

2 to 3 green onions, including tops, chopped

Optional additions: $1\,1/2$ cups chopped cooked meats or fish; chopped vegetables such as bell peppers, zucchini, celery, carrots, jicama, tomatoes; olives; nuts; fruit such as oranges, pears, and apples

In a large mixing or serving bowl combine the oil, vinegar, mustard (if using), garlic, and salt and pepper to taste and stir to mix. Add the rice, green onions, and selected additions and mix well. Let stand for 20 minutes for flavors to blend.

WILD RICE SALAD WITH PECANS AND ORANGES

Prepare the master recipe using wild rice and the following changes: Substitute walnut oil for the olive oil and use white wine vinegar or a flavored vinegar. Proceed as directed and stir in 1/2 cup toasted pecans; 1 orange, sectioned and chopped; and 1/2 cup chopped fresh parsley. Optionally, add 1/4 pound cooked small or medium shrimp, shelled and deveined, coarsely chopped.

BROWN RICE ENERGY SALAD

Prepare the master recipe using brown rice and these changes: Make the dressing with 1/3 cup olive oil and 3 tablespoons rice vinegar or 1/2 cup fat-free salad dressing. Stir into the rice 3 green onions, including the green tops, chopped; 1 tablespoon miso (omit if using prepared salad dressing); 1 carrot, grated; 1 celery stalk, chopped; 1 small apple, chopped; and 1 cup cooked beans or cubed firm tofu. Stir in 1/2 cup toasted walnuts or 2 tablespoons toasted sesame seeds.

BORDELAISE RICE SALAD

Prepare the master recipe using white rice and these changes: Make the dressing with porcini- or other mushroom-flavored oil and white wine vinegar. Stir in 1 tablespoon fines herbes. Stir into the rice 1 carrot, finely chopped; 1/2 onion, finely chopped; 1 celery stalk, finely chopped; and 1/2 cup sliced mushrooms. Add more oil and vinegar if needed because the mushrooms will soak up the liquid. Garnish with wedges of marinated artichoke hearts and chopped fresh parsley.

MILANESE RICE SALAD

Prepare the master recipe using white or brown rice, with these changes: Make the dressing with 1/3 cup olive oil, 2 tablespoons red wine vinegar, 1 teaspoon garlic paste, and 1/4 cup marinara or other Italian pasta sauce. Add to the rice 1/2 cup sliced mushrooms, 5 to 6 marinated artichoke hearts or 1/2 cup of giardiniera or other pickled vegetables, 6 to 8 pitted kalamata olives, and 3 to 4 ounces ham, cut into small rectangles or cubes. Garnish with chopped fresh basil.

CHINESE RICE SALAD

Prepare the master recipe using white rice. For the dressing, use canola or safflower oil plus 1 teaspoon toasted sesame oil and 3 tablespoons rice vinegar. Proceed as directed and add to the rice $1/2$ carrot, grated; a handful of blanched snow peas; $1/2$ orange, sectioned and cut into bite-sized pieces; and 1 to 2 tablespoons toasted cashews.

MEXICAN RICE SALAD

Prepare the master recipe using white or brown rice. For the dressing, use corn oil and white wine vinegar. Add to the rice $1/2$ cup cooked black beans; $1/2$ cup cooked corn kernels; $1/2$ cup salsa; and $1/2$ avocado, cubed and sprinkled with fresh lime juice. One-half pound of cooked ground beef can also be stirred in. Garnish with chopped fresh cilantro.

CURRIED RICE SALAD

Prepare the master recipe using white or brown rice, safflower or canola oil, and white wine vinegar. Before proceeding, warm the oil in a skillet over medium heat. Sauté the green onions until just softened, about 3 minutes. Stir in 1 to 2 tablespoons curry powder or paste and sauté 1 minute longer. Mix the onions with the vinegar, mustard, and garlic in a salad bowl and toss with the rice. Add 1 grated carrot; $1/2$ red bell pepper, seeded and chopped; 1 to 2 tablespoons raisins; and $1/2$ of a mango or apple, chopped. Garnish with chopped fresh cilantro and serve with chutney.

CLASSIC POTATO SALAD

serves 6 to 8

The secret to making a good potato salad is to toss the cooked potatoes in some vinegar or wine and onions or garlic as soon as they are cool enough to handle.

6 large white rose or new potatoes (2 3/4 to 3 pounds)

4 to 6 tablespoons vinegar or white wine

4 to 5 green onions, including green tops, chopped

2 garlic cloves, minced, or 1 teaspoon garlic paste

Salt and freshly ground black or white pepper

1/2 to 3/4 cup plain or flavored mayonnaise

1/4 cup canola, safflower, or olive oil

1 to 2 tablespoons hot-sweet, Dijon-style, tarragon, garlic, whole grain, or other prepared mustard, or 2 teaspoons dry mustard

2 to 4 tablespoons milk, sour cream, or plain yogurt

1 onion, finely chopped

2 celery stalks, chopped

1 carrot, grated (optional)

2 hard-cooked eggs (optional)

Paprika

Optional additions: sliced olives; bell pepper, seeded and chopped; capers; pesto; red pepper relish; tuna

Place the potatoes in a large pot and cover with water by 1 or 2 inches. Bring to a boil and cook until tender, about 25 minutes. When cool enough to handle, peel if desired. Otherwise cube or slice them with their peels on.

(continued at right)

In a bowl, combine the vinegar, green onions, garlic, salt and pepper, and immediately pour over the warm potatoes. In a small bowl, combine the mayonnaise and oil with the mustard and milk to make the dressing. When the potatoes are cool, stir in the onion, celery, and carrot. Mix well. Pour in the dressing and mix to coat. If the salad is dry, add a little milk or more vinegar. Top with sliced hard-cooked eggs (if using) and sprinkle with paprika.

CLASSIC POTATO SALAD WITH DRESSING

Prepare the master recipe with these changes: For the oil, vinegar, mayonnaise, mustard, and milk, substitute 1 to 1½ cups oil-based salad dressing — either the master recipe (page 94) or a prepared dressing flavored with basil, cumin, ginger, or other herb or spice. Toss half of the dressing with the warm potatoes as soon as possible. When potatoes are cooked, stir in onion, celery, carrot, and more dressing, then garnish.

MUSTARD POTATO SALAD

Prepare the master recipe and add ¼ cup yellow or flavored mustard to the dressing ingredients.

CURRIED POTATO SALAD

Prepare the master recipe with these changes: Add curry paste to taste. Substitute plain yogurt for the mayonnaise. Include chopped red bell peppers. Optional additions include ½ cup golden raisins and ½ cup toasted slivered almonds cooked, stir in onion, celery, carrot, and more dressing, then garnish.

SLICED and COOKED POTATO SALAD

serves 4 to 6

I learned this technique for making potato salad from Maggie Waldron, who published her method in *Potatoes: A Country Garden Cookbook*. Potatoes are sliced before cooking, so they are recipe-ready in minutes and each slice is cooked evenly.

6 medium red potatoes, sliced $1/4$ inch thick

$1/2$ cup white wine or prepared salad dressing

1 to 2 garlic cloves, minced, or $1/2$ to 1 teaspoon garlic paste

$1/4$ cup vegetable or olive oil

Salt and freshly ground black or white pepper

Optional additions: mustard, herbs, fresh parsley or mint, capers, tomatoes, onions

Put the potatoes in a saucepan with a tight-fitting lid. Cover with water by about 1 inch. Cover and bring to a boil and cook until tender, 15 to 20 minutes. Drain in a colander and toss with the wine and garlic while warm. Add oil and sprinkle with salt and pepper to taste.

SLICED POTATO SALAD WITH DRESSING

Cook the potatoes as directed in the master recipe. Toss them with $1/2$ to $3/4$ cup favorite prepared or homemade salad dressing. Add other ingredients that complement the flavors, such as chopped red or green bell peppers; chopped green onions; grated carrot; marinated artichoke hearts; sliced mushrooms.

NIÇOISE POTATO SALAD

Cook the potatoes as directed in the master recipe. For the dressing, combine $1/2$ cup olive oil, 2 tablespoons fresh lemon juice, and 2 to 4 tablespoons red wine vinegar. Stir in 1 teaspoon fines herbes, salad herbs, or herbes de Provence. Toss with the potatoes. Add 2 to 3 tomatoes, quartered; 3 green onions, including green tops, chopped; Niçoise olives; 1 to 2 tablespoons capers; and 2 to 3 ounces canned, grilled, or smoked tuna. Garnish with wedges of hard-cooked egg, blanched green beans, and chopped fresh parsley.

GERMAN POTATO SALAD

Cook the potatoes as directed in the master recipe. For the dressing, toss $2/3$ to $3/4$ cup prepared creamy salad dressing with the potatoes. Stir in 3 chopped green onions, including the green tops; $1/2$ red bell pepper, seeded and chopped (or $1/3$ cup chopped pimiento); and 2 to 3 ounces crisply fried bacon or ham. Garnish with chopped fresh parsley.

PERUVIAN POTATO SALAD

This version is inspired by Patti and Javier at Bodega Goat Cheese in Sonoma County, California. Cook the potatoes as directed in the master recipe. For the dressing, in a blender or food processor, puree 2 to 3 ounces creamy goat cheese, $1/4$ cup oil, 2 to 3 tablespoons white wine vinegar, 2 to 4 tablespoons plain yogurt, 1 teaspoon garlic paste, $1/3$ cup red pepper spread, and chile paste to taste. Thin with more yogurt or milk if necessary. Toss with the cooked potatoes and garnish with chopped fresh basil or parsley. Alternatively, use the sauce as a dip for cooked potatoes and other vegetables.

PASTA SALAD
serves 4 to 6

I try to combine a flavored pasta with a compatible oil or vinegar. For example, I might dress a salad made with zinfandel-flavored pasta shaped like a cluster of grapes with roasted garlic olive oil from the Napa Valley and zinfandel vinegar, then toss all with fresh grapes or raisins. Or, enhance the zing of chile-flecked tagliarini noodles with a prepared Asian-style dressing or Mexican salsa in a vinaigrette.

1 teaspoon salt

1/2 pound dried pasta noodles

1/2 cup olive, canola, or safflower oil

2 to 4 tablespoons vinegar

1 to 3 garlic cloves, or 1/2 to 3 teaspoons garlic paste or roasted garlic paste

3 to 4 green onions, including green tops, chopped

Salt and freshly ground black or white pepper

Optional additions: grated carrot, chopped marinated artichoke hearts, pitted olives, toasted pine nuts, chopped red and/or green bell pepper, chopped shallots, fresh or dried herbs

In a large stock pot bring at least 3 quarts of water to boil. Add the salt and the noodles and cook until quite tender. Drain in a colander and rinse under running cold water to cool and stop cooking. In a large bowl whisk together the oil, vinegar, garlic, and onions. Add salt and pepper to taste and stir in the noodles. Toss well and add other ingredients as you like.

THAI NOODLE SALAD

Use linguine or spaghetti and cook as directed in the master recipe. To the dressing ingredients add 1 tablespoon tomato paste, $1/2$ teaspoon (or to taste) chile paste with garlic, 1 teaspoon sugar, 1 to 2 tablespoons fish sauce, and $1/4$ cup fresh lime juice. Toss the dressing with the noodles and add $1/2$ carrot, grated, and 2 or 3 Roma tomatoes, cut into wedges. Garnish with chopped fresh basil leaves (or whole basil leaves fried in a little oil) and $1/2$ cup chopped roasted peanuts.

PESTO PASTA SALAD

Use tiny tubes, shells, or an herb-flavored or shaped pasta and cook as directed in the master recipe. To the dressing ingredients add $1/2$ to $3/4$ cup pesto and extra garlic, if you like. Optionally, stir in 2 to 3 tablespoons mayonnaise. Taste for seasoning and toss with the noodles. Stir in $1/2$ cup coarsely chopped pitted olives; $1/2$ red bell pepper, seeded and chopped; and $1/2$ cup chopped fresh basil leaves. In addition, $1/4$ to $1/2$ pound shelled and deveined cooked shrimp may be added.

TOMATO LINGUINE SALAD

Use linguine or spaghetti and cook as directed in the master recipe. For the dressing, use olive oil and 2 to 3 tablespoons balsamic vinegar or 4 tablespoons tomato-infused vinegar. Stir in 1 tablespoon grated lemon zest, 1 teaspoon garlic paste, and 3 to 4 tablespoons Italian herb blend. Season with salt and pepper to taste. Toss with the noodles and stir in 10 black or green olives, pitted and chopped; 1 red bell pepper, seeded and sliced; and 5 tomatoes, seeded and chopped. If you like, toss in $1/2$ pound of cooked small or medium shrimp, shelled and deveined. Garnish with chopped fresh parsley.

CHINESE SESAME NOODLE SALAD

Use fresh Chinese noodles or dried spaghetti and cook as directed in the master recipe. For the dressing, use safflower or canola oil and rice vinegar. Add 1 1/2 teaspoons toasted sesame oil, 1 teaspoon (or more to taste) hot oil, and 2 teaspoons soy sauce. (In place of the dressing you may substitute 1/2 cup, or more to taste, bottled Chinese salad dressing.) Toss with the noodles and add 1/2 cup chopped red or green bell pepper; 1 cup blanched snow peas, peas, or broccoli florets; 1/3 cup toasted sesame seeds; and 1 cup bean sprouts (optional). In addition, 1 cup cubed, cooked chicken or cooked small or medium shrimp, shelled and deveined, can be added. Garnish with chopped fresh parsley or cilantro.

SZECHUAN NOODLE SALAD

Prepare Chinese Sesame Noodle Salad (preceding) except for the dressing. In the bowl, combine 2 to 3 tablespoons Szechuan sauce, 1/4 cup safflower or canola oil, and 2 tablespoons rice vinegar.

PANTRY
TIP

Use inexpensive, quick-rehydrating ramen noodles
(toss out their salty seasoning packets) for the
Thai, Chinese, or Szechuan Noodle Salad, or Tomato Linguine Salad.
Boil 2 cups of water per 3 ounces of noodles.
Cook the noodles for about 2 minutes.
Drain, rinse, and dress with favorite dressing.

PANTRY
EQUIVALENTS

SALAD DRESSING

$1/3$ to $1/2$ cup dressing is enough for 1 average head of lettuce

$3/4$ cup dressing is enough for 8 cups raw cabbage; $2/3$ cup for 8 cups hot slaw

$1/2$ cup dressing is enough for 4 cups cooked rice
(more may be needed if rice soaks up the dressing)

1 to $1^1/2$ cups dressing is enough for 3 pounds ($5^1/2$ cups) of potato salad
(more may be needed if potatoes soak up the dressing)

$1/2$ to $3/4$ cup dressing is enough for $1/2$ pound (3 to 4 cups) cooked pasta

$1/3$ to $1/2$ cup dressing is enough for 4 cups beans or legumes

LETTUCE

1 head red or other leaf lettuce equals 4 to 6 first-course or 2 to 3 entrée salads

1 head romaine lettuce equals 6 to 8 first-course or 4 entrée salads

1 head butter or Boston bibb lettuce equals 4 first-course or 2 entrée salads

1 bunch spinach equals 6 to 8 first-course or 4 entrée salads

One 10-ounce package of prewashed and cut lettuce equals about 6 cups

Use $1^1/2$ cups or about 2 ounces of lettuce per portion for first-course,
$2^1/2$ cups for an entrée salad

POTATOES

One 8-ounce potato equals 2 cups cubed or coarsely chopped and
$2^1/2$ cups grated potatoes (and squeezed of excess moisture) equals 1 cup mashed

2 medium russet or white rose potatoes equals 1 pound

3 medium red potatoes equals 1 pound

3 pounds potatoes equals $5^1/2$ cups cubed potatoes or
6 to 8 servings potato salad

BEAN SALAD

serves 6 to 8

Sticking to the traditional black, red, white, lima, and Great Northern beans means you can buy them in cans to make a salad in minutes. Shopping for beans in specialty stores (see Sources, page 255) turns up dried varieties with exotic flavors, colors, textures, and patterns, but unlike canned beans, they must be cooked before you can use them. With their earthy texture and bulk, beans warrant all the gusto today's saucemakers can devise. If you are going to combine several varieties of beans in one dish, each must be cooked separately. Soaking beans for several hours or overnight lessens their cooking time (see Pot of Beans, page 126, for soaking and cooking directions).

$1/3$ **cup canola, safflower, or olive oil**

3 to 4 tablespoons vinegar

1 to 3 garlic cloves, minced or chopped, or $1/2$ to $1^1/2$ teaspoons garlic paste

Salt and freshly ground black pepper

$4^1/2$ to 5 cups cooked beans ($3/4$ pound dried), or three

15-ounce cans beans, drained and rinsed

$1/2$ **onion,** chopped

$1/2$ **red or green bell pepper,** seeded and chopped

Optional additions: chopped whole green onions, sliced olives, crumbled feta cheese, small cubes of Cheddar cheese, chopped nuts

In a large salad bowl, whisk together the oil, vinegar, garlic, and salt and pepper. Toss with the cooked or canned beans, then stir in the onion, bell pepper, and any other ingredients you are using.
Adjust seasoning to taste.

SOUTH-OF-THE-BORDER BEAN SALAD

Prepare the master recipe using red or black beans. Combine the dressing ingredients as directed and add 1/2 cup salsa. Into the beans, stir 3 Roma tomatoes, chopped; 1 cooked cup corn kernels (unless you are using a salsa with corn in it); and chopped fresh cilantro to taste. Top with cubes of avocado that have been drizzled with fresh lime or lemon juice and serve with additional salsa.

MIDDLE EASTERN LENTIL SALAD

Prepare the master recipe using cooked lentils (they take 25 to 30 minutes to cook). Combine the dressing ingredients with 1 to 3 teaspoons Middle Eastern spice blend. Stir in ajvar (to taste; it is hot), 2 tablespoons red pepper spread or tomato paste, and the juice of 1 lemon. Toss with the lentils and, in addition to the red bell pepper and onion in the master recipe, add 3 green onions, including green tops, chopped; and 1 cup chopped fresh parsley.

NORTH AFRICAN GARBANZO SALAD

Prepare the master recipe using garbanzo beans (also called ceci or chickpeas). Use olive oil and a flavored white wine vinegar, and add 1 to 4 tablespoons harissa. Toss the dressing with the beans, and in addition to the green bell pepper and onion in the master recipe, add 3 tomatoes, chopped; and the juice of 1 lemon. Top with chopped fresh cilantro and toasted sesame seeds.

CAJUN BLACK-EYED PEA SALAD

Prepare the master recipe using black-eyed peas. For the dressing use 2/3 to 3/4 cup Cajun-style dressing (or to make your own, combine 1/3 cup pecan or olive oil, 3 to 4 tablespoons red wine vinegar, 1 additional teaspoon garlic paste, 1 tablespoon hot-sweet or Cajun-style mustard, and salt and pepper to taste). Toss the dressing with the black-eyed peas and, in addition to the onion and red or green bell pepper, add 3 green onions, including green tops, chopped; 1/2 cup chopped fresh parsley; and 4 to 5 Roma tomatoes, chopped.

ITALIAN BEAN SALAD

For this classic antipasto, prepare the master recipe using a combination of red beans and garbanzo beans, cooked separately. Mix the dressing as directed or use $2/3$ to $3/4$ cup of a favorite bottled Italian dressing and toss with the beans. Stir in more garlic, 1 to 3 teaspoons Italian herb blend, and chopped fresh parsley.

PECAN, WHITE BEAN, AND BASIL SALAD

Prepare the master recipe using Great Northern beans and omit the onion and bell pepper. For the dressing, combine $1/2$ cup pecan or walnut oil, 2 tablespoons sherry vinegar, 1 to 2 tablespoons white wine vinegar, 2 to 3 tablespoons hot-sweet mustard, $1 1/2$ teaspoons garlic paste, and salt and freshly ground black pepper to taste. Toss with the beans, and stir in 3 green onions, including green tops, chopped; 2 tomatoes, chopped; and 1 bunch of fresh basil leaves, chopped (or $1/2$ cup pesto).

PANTRY
TIPS

Freshen commercial salad dressings by stirring in chopped
tomatoes, shallots, green onions, or garlic.

If a vinaigrette-type dressing or sauce is being used
to dress green vegetables, toss them together at the last moment
to maintain the color as long as possible.

vegetables +

beans

THREE

Think of **VEGETABLES** and **BEANS** as bases similar

to grains such as pasta, rice, and polenta, and sauce

and season them similarly. These recipes are for single

vegetables or for specific combinations designed

to introduce a world of flavors. Basically, vegetables are

steamed, sautéed, baked, roasted, or boiled and

then sauced, so experiment to find your signature dish

or momentary favorite.

**Mixed
Vegetable Sauté**
page 118

Roasted Vegetables
page 120

RECIPE
LIST

Stuffed Potatoes
page 122

Dinnercakes
page 134

Stuffed Eggplant
page 130

Pot of Beans
page 126

MIXED VEGETABLE SAUTÉ

serves 4 to 6

Just like stir-frying, this is a fast way to get some vegetables on the table when everyone is in a hurry to eat. Adding meat, fish, poultry, or eggs makes a vegetable dish like this into a main course. Or you can add more sauce to the vegetables alone and serve them over rice, pasta, or polenta. Thai, stir-fry, and Chinese seasonings, curry pastes and powders, herb blends, and marinades are some of my suggestions to add to this sauté. Plan on 1 cup or so of cubed or cut-up vegetables per person to make a side dish, 2 to 3 cups for an entrée.

2 to 3 tablespoons vegetable or olive oil

1/2 onion, chopped or sliced

2 garlic cloves, minced, or 1 teaspoon garlic paste

1 to 3 tablespoons herb or spice blend

6 cups assorted coarsely cut, cubed, or sliced vegetables such

as eggplant, bell peppers, carrots, peeled daikon radish, peeled turnips, squash, peeled sweet potatoes, leek tops, mushrooms, tomatoes

1/2 to 3/4 cup canned broth or sauce such as stewed tomatoes, pasta sauce, curry sauce, stir-fry sauce

Chopped fresh parsley or basil, for garnish

In a nonstick skillet over medium heat, warm the oil. Sauté the onion until softened. Add the garlic, and herbs or spices and cook 1 minute. Stir in first the vegetables that take longest to cook such as eggplant, peppers, carrots, and turnips. Then add the broth or sauce and cook on medium-high heat 3 to 5 minutes before adding quicker-cooking vegetables like squash, sweet potatoes, and leeks. Simmer another few minutes until everything is tender and the liquid is reduced and thickened. Garnish with parsley or basil.

ASIAN VEGETABLE STIR-FRY

Prepare the master recipe with these changes: Substitute 1 tablespoon chopped peeled ginger for the herbs. For the broth, use $1/4$ to $1/2$ cup stir-fry sauce, Szechuan sauce, or Korean bol goki sauce plus water to dilute if the sauce is too salty. Include $1/2$ pound bean sprouts with your choice of vegetables. Serve with soy sauce or tamari if you like.

MEXICAN VEGETABLE STIR-FRY

Prepare the master recipe with these changes: When the garlic is added also add 1 tablespoon Mexican herb blend. Then, stir in vegetables such as zucchini, summer squash, red and green bell peppers, chayote, and corn kernels. For the liquid, use salsa, or enchilada sauce diluted with water. Serve garnished with chopped fresh cilantro, chopped avocado, and lime wedges if desired.

CURRIED VEGETABLE STIR-FRY

Prepare the master recipe with these changes: When the garlic is added, stir in 1 to 2 tablespoons curry powder or 2 to 4 tablespoons curry paste. Then stir in the vegetables of choice. Use stock, water, or coconut milk for the liquid. Garnish with grated unsweetened coconut and chopped fresh parsley or cilantro.

PEANUT-VEGETABLE STIR-FRY

Prepare the master recipe with these changes: Substitute $1/2$ cup Indonesian or Thai peanut sauce for the broth. Garnish with chopped roasted peanuts.

POLYNESIAN VEGETABLE STIR-FRY

Prepare the master recipe, substituting one of the following sauces for the liquid: Polynesian-style, Hawaiian-style curry, stir-fry, pineapple-teriyaki, or sweet-and-sour. Taste the sauce before using and thin with water or broth if too salty or spicy. Add $1/4$ to $1/2$ cup of chopped fresh pineapple to the vegetable combination if you like.

KUNG PAO VEGETABLE STIR-FRY

Prepare the master recipe using vegetables of choice. Stir in kung pao sauce to taste and thin with stock, broth, or water if necessary. Garnish with slivers of fried garlic.

ROASTED VEGETABLES

serves 4

This fuss-free technique is my favorite way to cook vegetables –
especially potatoes. Season them with herb blends, garlic powder or
garlic blends, curry powder, spicy dry barbecue rubs, or Indian sambal
pastes. I roast all the vegetables at the same time, which means some,
such as tomatoes, get fall-apart tender and blend in like a sauce. When you pile the
roasted vegetables on a plate and sprinkle them with a fresh green herb, their
flavors merge beautifully. The amount of vegetables may sound like a lot, but the
volume tends to shrink when cooked at a high heat like this.

8 to 10 cups quartered or chunked vegetables (have pieces about the same size) such as potatoes, peeled sweet potatoes, peeled yams, onions, bell peppers, zucchini, yellow squash, peeled turnips, peeled rutabagas, carrots, tomatoes, mushrooms, and eggplant

1/4 cup olive oil or flavored oil

4 to 5 garlic cloves, minced, or 2 to 3 teaspoons garlic paste

Salt and freshly ground black pepper

Garnish: minced fresh parsley, chives, marjoram, and/or basil

**Preheat the oven to 425 degrees F. Toss the prepared vegetables in a
bowl with the oil, garlic, and salt and pepper. Spread them in a
single layer on a rimmed baking sheet. Roast for 30 to 40 minutes,
stirring occasionally so the vegetables brown on all sides. When
the vegetables are tender, remove from the oven and place in a
serving dish. Sprinkle with fresh herbs and serve.**

ITALIAN ROASTED VEGETABLES

Prepare the master recipe and add 2 to 3 tablespoons Italian herb blend to the oil and garlic before mixing with the vegetables. Garnish with chopped fresh basil or parsley.

CURRIED ROASTED VEGETABLES

Prepare the master recipe and add 2 to 3 tablespoons curry powder to the oil and garlic before mixing with the vegetables.

SOUTH-OF-THE-BORDER ROASTED VEGETABLES

Prepare the master recipe and add 2 tablespoons chili powder, Mexican, or Southwestern herb blend to the oil and garlic before mixing with the potatoes. Garnish with chopped fresh cilantro.

ZA'ATAR-SPICED ROASTED VEGETABLES

Prepare the master recipe and add 2 to 3 tablespoons za'atar to the oil and garlic before mixing with the potatoes. Garnish with chopped fresh cilantro, or a mixture of chopped fresh mint leaves and lemon zest.

PANTRY
TIPS

As a dip for artichokes or other vegetables, combine 1 cup plain mayonnaise with 1 to 2 tablespoons lemon- or herb-flavored vinegar, 1/2 teaspoon garlic paste or garlic-and-herb blend, and a little ground black or white pepper.

As a dip for vegetables (or shrimp, or to dollop on pizza), make this Quick Aioli: Combine 1/2 cup homemade or commercial mayonnaise with 1 to 2 teaspoons garlic paste or roasted garlic paste. Stir in a squeeze or so of fresh lemon juice and let stand at least 30 minutes for flavors to blend.

STUFFED POTATOES

serves 4

If your oven has a programmable feature that turns it on and off at a preset time, you can come home to the smell of freshly baking potatoes and a delicious base for making a meal. The potatoes can also be stuffed a day in advance and held in the refrigerator.

4 medium to large russet potatoes (about 8 ounces each)

4 tablespoons butter

1/2 to 3/4 cup milk

Salt and ground black or white pepper

Paprika

Preheat the oven to 400 degrees F. Scrub the potatoes in cold water, then bake until very soft, about 45 minutes. When the baked potatoes are cool enough to handle, halve them lengthwise. Scoop the potato out of the skins and place it in a bowl. Lay the skins on a baking sheet. Mash the potatoes with a fork or potato masher. Add the butter and milk and stir until the potatoes are creamy. Season with salt and pepper to taste. Spoon the potatoes back into their skins and sprinkle with paprika. Reduce the oven temperature to 375 degrees F and bake until the tops are crisped and potatoes are heated through, about 10 minutes.
If the potatoes were stuffed ahead, and are cold, they will take about 20 minutes to reheat.

ITALIAN STUFFED POTATOES

Bake the potatoes as directed in the master recipe. After the potato has been scooped out of the skins and mashed, mix with 4 tablespoons of butter and $1/2$ cup milk. Stir in $1/2$ to $3/4$ cup chopped fresh arugula or spinach; 3 Roma tomatoes, chopped; and $1/2$ cup grated Parmesan cheese. Add salt and pepper to taste. Return the filling to the skins and sprinkle a tablespoon or so of toasted pine nuts over the tops and bake for 8 to 10 minutes as directed. Top with chopped fresh basil, arugula, or parsley.

MEXICAN STUFFED POTATOES

Bake the potatoes as directed in the master recipe. After the potato has been scooped out of the skins and mashed, add 2 tablespoons butter and $1/2$ cup milk. Stir in $1/2$ cup grated Cheddar cheese and $1/2$ cup salsa. Optional additions include 2 green onions, including green tops, chopped; $1/4$ cup sliced olives; $1/4$ cup chopped fresh cilantro; 3 Roma tomatoes, diced; $1/2$ pound cooked ground beef or sausage. Add salt and pepper to taste. After the second baking, top with chopped fresh cilantro and cubes of avocado, if desired, before serving.

GARLIC-HERB STUFFED POTATOES

Bake the potatoes as directed in the master recipe. After the potato has been scooped out of the skins and mashed, add 4 tablespoons butter, 2 to 3 teaspoons roasted garlic paste, 2 teaspoons favorite herb blend, and 1 to 2 teaspoons snipped fresh chives. Stir in $1/3$ to $1/2$ cup milk and spoon back into the potato skins. Bake again, then garnish with more chopped chives or chopped fresh parsley.

SHEPHERD'S STUFFED POTATOES

Bake the potatoes as directed in the master recipe. While the potatoes are baking, brown $1/2$ pound ground lamb and pour off all grease. After the potato has been scooped out of the skins and mashed, add 4 tablespoons butter, 1 teaspoon roasted garlic paste, 1 tablespoon snipped fresh chives, and $1/3$ to $1/2$ cup milk. Season with salt and pepper to taste. Spoon back into the skins, sprinkle with paprika, and bake as directed. Garnish with snipped fresh chives or chopped fresh parsley.

COLCANNON-STUFFED POTATOES

Bake the potatoes as directed in the master recipe. While the potatoes are baking, finely chop 1/2 small head of green cabbage and 4 green onions, including green tops. Sauté them in 2 tablespoons safflower or canola oil or butter and sprinkle with salt and pepper. After the potato has been scooped out of the skins and mashed, add 4 tablespoons butter, 1/2 teaspoon roasted garlic paste, 1/2 cup milk, and the cabbage mixture. Add salt and pepper to taste. Spoon the mixture back into the skins, sprinkle with paprika, and bake as directed. Garnish with chopped green onion tops or chopped fresh parsley.

MUSHROOM-STUFFED POTATOES

Bake the potatoes as directed in the master recipe. While the potatoes are baking, in a skillet over medium heat, warm 3 tablespoons butter and sauté 1 cup sliced mushrooms and 2 chopped green onions, including green tops, until softened, about 4 minutes. Grate 1/2 cup fontina, Swiss, Monterey Jack, or other semi-hard cheese. Combine with the mashed potatoes and stir gently to mix. Spoon the mixture back into the skins, sprinkle with paprika, and bake as directed. Garnish with chopped green onion tops or chopped fresh parsley.

PANTRY
EQUIVALENTS

VEGETABLES

1 medium onion equals 6 ounces or 2 cups chopped

1 cup cubed or coarsely chopped sautéed vegetables equals 1 serving

1 medium tomato equals 4 ounces or $3/4$ cup chopped

1 ear of corn equals $3/4$ cup kernels

8 ounces button mushrooms equals $2^1/2$ cups sliced

$1^1/2$ to 2 cups cubed or coarsely chopped roasted vegetables equals 1 serving

10 ounces frozen corn kernels equals $1^1/4$ cups

1 small zucchini equals 6 ounces or $1^1/2$ to 2 cups cubed

1 medium carrot equals 1 cup grated

1 large eggplant equals $1^3/4$ to 2 pounds or 8 cups cubed

1 Roma tomato equals 2 ounces or $1/4$ cup chopped

BEANS

12 ounces ($3/4$ pound) dried beans equals approximately 4 cups cooked
or 6 to 8 servings

One 16-ounce can equals 2 cups cooked beans

1 pound ($2^1/4$ cups) of dried lentils equals 5 cups cooked or
6 to 8 servings

POT of BEANS

serves 6 to 8

Cooking a pot of beans takes an hour or two depending on the beans. Try some of the incredible varieties of beans on the market today. Colors, sizes, and names such as appaloosa, rattlesnake, calypso, trout, snowcap, and scarlet emperor make beans intriguing to cook, talk about, and, best of all, to eat. See Sources, page 255, for suppliers. All the recipes use cooked beans, so canned may be substituted. When cooking dried beans never add anything acidic, such as tomatoes, until the beans are tender. The acid stops the cooking and the beans will remain hard if you add the acid too soon. If you are combining more than one type of bean in a recipe, cook each separately.

1 pound dried beans (approximately 6 cups cooked)

Wash the beans in a colander and pick them over to remove any that are damaged. Soak them overnight in water to cover by 2 inches, or do a quick soak by putting them in a pot, covering them with water by 2 inches, and bringing them to a boil. Then turn off the burner and let them soak for an hour. Drain. In a large pot, combine the beans with water to cover by 2 inches. Bring to a boil and reduce the heat to medium-high. Partially cover and cook until tender, 45 minutes to 2 hours, depending on the bean. Add more water if necessary. Don't drain them; you may need some of the liquid for the recipe.

QUICK CHILI

Scoop 3 cups cooked beans (kidney, red, black, black-eyed peas, or any other bean) out of their liquid (or drain and rinse if canned) and place in a saucepan. Stir in $2/3$ cup barbecue sauce plus 1 to 2 cups bean liquid or water and bring to a boil. Mix in $1 1/2$ teaspoons bean herb blend and add $1/2$ pound chopped cooked beef or pork, or $1/2$ pound browned ground beef or cubed meat loaf, if you like. Cook the chili over medium heat for 5 to 10 minutes to blend flavors. Garnish with grated Cheddar cheese and chopped green onions or fresh cilantro.

WESTERN BAKED BEANS

Preheat oven to 350 degrees F. Scoop 6 cups cooked beans (red or small white) out of their liquid (or drain and rinse if canned) and place in an ovenproof casserole or baking dish. Stir in 1 to 2 tablespoons bean herb blend, 1 teaspoon garlic paste, 2 tablespoons molasses, 2 tablespoons hot-sweet mustard, and 1 cup tomato sauce. If liquid doesn't cover beans by $1/2$ inch, ladle in some of the bean cooking liquid. Bake, uncovered, until bubbling, 20 to 30 minutes.

MEXICAN BAKED BEANS

Preheat oven to 350 degrees F. Scoop 6 cups cooked beans (red, pinto, or a specialty) out of their liquid (or drain and rinse if canned) and place in an ovenproof casserole or baking dish. In a skillet, warm 2 tablespoons canola or safflower oil over medium heat. Sauté 1 onion, chopped; 2 green bell peppers, seeded and chopped; 1 to 2 table-spoons Mexican herb blend; and 1 teaspoon garlic paste until softened. Stir the mixture into the beans and add $1 1/2$ cups enchilada sauce, 1 cup coarsely chopped olives, and one $3 1/2$-ounce can ($1/2$ cup) chopped green chiles. Mix well and bake until heated through, 20 to 30 minutes. Garnish with chopped fresh cilantro. These can be used in Polenta Tamale Pie (page 144).

BRAZILIAN BAKED BEANS

Preheat oven to 350 degrees F. Scoop 6 cups cooked beans (red or white) out of their liquid (or drain and rinse if canned) and place in an ovenproof casserole or baking dish. In skillet, fry ½ pound slab bacon, finely diced, until crisp. Drain off fat. (Alternatively, start the recipe here if you don't want to add the bacon.) Warm 2 tablespoons canola or safflower oil in the pan. Sauté 1 large red onion, chopped. Stir in 1 tablespoon garlic paste and 2 tablespoons dry or prepared mustard and 1 teaspoon chile paste or crushed red pepper and cook for 1 minute. Add 3 cups cold coffee, ³/4 cup molasses, and salt to taste. Bring the mixture to a boil and pour over the beans. Cover and bake, stirring occasionally, until thickened, 40 to 50 minutes.

MIDDLE EASTERN GARBANZOS

In a skillet, warm 2 tablespoons olive oil. Sauté 1 onion, chopped, until softened. Stir in 2 to 4 tablespoons ajvar and 1 cup tomato sauce. Put the mixture in a large pot and add 3 cups cooked garbanzo beans (also called ceci beans or chickpeas), scooped out of their liquid (or drain and rinse if canned). Add 2 cups chopped spinach (one 10-ounce package frozen chopped spinach, thawed) and 2 tablespoons tahini. Bring just to a boil. Stir in the juice of 1 lemon and salt and pepper to taste, then serve. Garnish with chopped tomatoes, chopped cucumber, and yogurt, and serve in pita bread, if you like.

BASQUE THREE-BEAN STEW

For this version, use ³/4 cup each Great Northern, pinto, and red beans, cooked separately (or use 6 cups of one type only). In a skillet, sauté 1 pound chorizo sausage (casing removed). Pour off grease and remove meat with a slotted spoon to a paper towel. In the same skillet, heat 5 tablespoons olive oil. Sauté 1 green and 1 red bell pepper, seeded and chopped; 2 onions, chopped; and 1½ tablespoons garlic paste, until softened. Scoop the cooked beans out of their liquid (or drain and rinse if canned) and combine them in one pot. Reserve the cooking liquid. Stir onion-pepper mixture and chorizo into the beans. Add reserved bean liquid or water to make it semi-soupy. Cook over medium-low heat, or until slightly thickened, 45 to 60 minutes. Just before serving, stir in 1 teaspoon garlic paste. Cook 5 minutes more.

Scoop 6 cups cooked black beans out of their liquid (or drain and rinse if canned) and place in a saucepan. In a skillet over medium heat, warm 2 tablespoons oil. Sauté 1 onion, chopped; 1 green bell pepper, seeded and chopped; and 1 tablespoon garlic paste until softened. Add Cuban or other Caribbean hot sauce to taste. Stir the mixture into the beans and cook over medium heat until flavors have blended, 20 to 30 minutes. Taste for seasoning. Add salt and pepper and more hot sauce if necessary. To serve, top with chopped avocado sprinkled with fresh lime juice or chopped papaya and chopped fresh cilantro.

STUFFED EGGPLANT

serves 4

Next to onions, the fat purple eggplant is the most universally popular vegetable. Sautéed, it handles the boldest sauces. Sliced and grilled, it is a pizza topping. And eggplant is terrific for stuffing. Select an umblemished firm eggplant for the best results. To eliminate the bitterness sometimes associated with eggplant, dice or slice the eggplant and sprinkle with salt. Set the eggplant pieces on paper towels for 20 minutes. Pat the "sweat" off with the paper towels and continue as directed in the recipe. Two methods are given for cooking whole eggplants: one will have texture and the other becomes a puree.

1 large globe eggplant

4 tablespoons olive, safflower, or canola oil

1 onion, chopped

2 garlic cloves, minced, or 1 teaspoon garlic paste or roasted garlic paste

Salt and ground black or white pepper

1/2 cup dried bread crumbs

Olive oil or oil in a spray can

Preheat the oven to 375 degrees F. Choose a variation. Prepare the eggplant following Method 1 or 2 – whichever the recipe specifies – then prepare the filling. Bake as directed in the master recipe.

METHOD 1 Halve the eggplant and score the flesh diagonally 3 times. Brush with 2 tablespoons of the oil and place, cut side down, on a baking sheet. Bake until soft, 25 to 35 minutes. Remove from oven. When cool enough to handle, remove the pulp with a knife or melon baller, being careful not to pierce the skin. Chop the pulp, place it in a bowl, and finish as directed in one of the following pantry selections.

METHOD 2 Cut the eggplant in half lengthwise and scoop out the flesh with a melon baller. In a skillet, heat 2 tablespoons of the oil and sauté the eggplant and onion until softened, 4 to 5 minutes. Add the garlic and sauté 20 seconds. Add salt and pepper to taste. Remove from heat, place in a bowl, and finish as directed in one of the following pantry selections.

To bake, stuff the eggplant mixture into the eggplant shells. Top with the bread crumbs and drizzle or spray the crumbs with the oil. Place on baking sheets and bake until heated through, 15 to 40 minutes (depending on method and filling).

MIDDLE EASTERN STUFFED EGGPLANT WITH TAHINI

Prepare the eggplant as directed in the master recipe, following Method 1 or 2 (Method 1 will produce a saucy texture, perfect to combine with pasta). Sauté the onion and the garlic, then stir in 1/3 cup tahini, the juice of 1 lemon, and 1/3 cup chopped fresh parsley. Mix with the eggplant. Season with salt and pepper to taste. Spoon the mixture into the eggplant shells and set on a baking sheet. Sprinkle with 1/2 cup dried bread crumbs and drizzle with 1 tablespoon olive oil (or spray with olive oil). Bake until heated through, 15 to 20 minutes (30 to 40 minutes if eggplant is done by Method 2). Serve with pita bread or Indian pappadam.

PROVENÇAL STUFFED EGGPLANT WITH LAMB

Prepare the eggplant as directed in the master recipe, following Method 2. Before sautéing the onion, brown 1 pound of lamb in a skillet. Pour off the fat in the skillet and add 1 tablespoon of olive oil, the eggplant, and the onion and garlic from the master recipe. Stir in 2 teaspoons herbes de Provence and 3 or 4 tomatoes, seeded and chopped. Season to taste with salt and pepper and more garlic if desired. Spoon the mixture into the eggplant shells and set them on a baking sheet. Sprinkle with 1/2 cup dried bread crumbs mixed with 2 teaspoons chopped fresh parsley or basil. Drizzle with olive oil (or spray with olive oil). Bake until heated through, 30 to 40 minutes.

JAPANESE STUFFED EGGPLANT WITH MISO

Prepare the eggplant as directed in the master recipe, following Method 1 or 2. Sauté the onion and garlic, then stir in 3/4 to 1 tablespoon miso and 1 to 2 teaspoons soy sauce or tamari, all to taste. Add 3 tablespoons toasted sesame seeds. Add ground black or red pepper or hot sauce to taste. Mix with the eggplant. Spoon the mixture into the eggplant shells and set on a baking sheet. Sprinkle with 1/2 cup dried bread crumbs and drizzle with 1 teaspoon toasted sesame oil. Bake until heated through, 15 to 20 minutes (30 to 40 minutes if eggplant is done by Method 2).

CAJUN BLACK BEAN CAKES

Follow the recipe for Black Bean Cakes (preceding) and add $1/4$ red and $1/4$ green bell pepper, seeded and finely chopped, and 1 to 2 teaspoons Cajun seasoning to the bean mixture before it is pureed. Makes about ten 3-inch cakes.

MIDDLE EASTERN TOPPING

Combine $1/2$ cup plain yogurt with 2 to 3 teaspoons za'atar and $1/4$ cup minced fresh parsley. Spoon over the cakes to taste. Makes about $3/4$ cup.

CHINESE PLUM SAUCE TOPPING

Top cakes with a spoonful of plain yogurt, then a dollop of Chinese plum sauce. Or, use the plum sauce alone.

PANTRY
TIPS

Glaze steamed vegetables with flavored butter:
Combine room-temperature butter with minced dried or fresh sage, thyme, or rosemary; ground cumin; garlic paste; grated Parmesan cheese; and/or other ingredients. Alternatively, use a commercially prepared butter glaze.

For Herbed Artichokes, add 1 to 2 tablespoons Italian or other herb blend and a teaspoon of olive oil to the water for cooking artichokes.

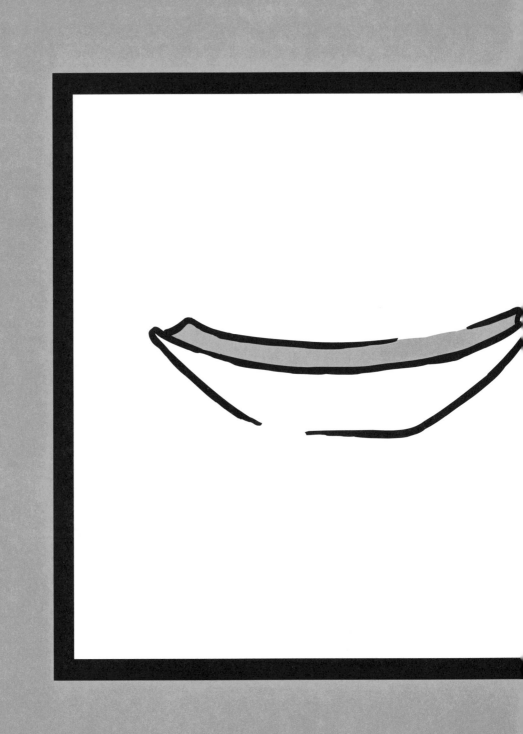

grains +

pasta

GRAINS and **PASTA** are the bases upon which to go wild with commercial sauces. You can stir in a mix of sun-dried tomatoes and herbs or add an olive salad to polenta and top it with a fresh-off-the-vine-tasting tomato sauce or richly concentrated mushroom sauce. Rice in all its varieties adds texture to sauces from every continent. Pasta from Asian, Italian, and American producers runs the gamut from quick-soaking rice noodles to wheat and buckwheat noodles, with whimsically shaped macaroni tossed in the pot for fun. The recipes here are an introduction to the possibilities.

Pasta and rice have long shelf lives. This and their amazing variety of flavors make them exceptionally important to stock in the pantry for nights when nothing is better then boiling up a comforting – or brazenly spicy – pot of noodles or rice.

Polenta

RECIPE
LIST

Pasta

Rice Cakes

Stove-top Rice

Baked Rice

**Skillet and
Stir-fried Rice**

POLENTA

serves 4

The coarse-grain cornmeal made popular by the Italians is one of my spur-of-the-minute company dishes as well as a weekly mainstay. I usually keep a roll of purchased polenta in the refrigerator to cut cooking time even further. Some commercial products are quite salty, so find one you like and stick with it. Here are two methods for cooking polenta.

4 cups water

1 cup polenta

$1/2$ teaspoon salt

STOVE-TOP METHOD In a medium saucepan, bring the water to a boil. Stir in the polenta and the salt and reduce the heat to medium. Cook, stirring frequently to keep from sticking, until all the water is absorbed and the texture is as you like. For a fine, creamy polenta, this will take up to 40 minutes. If you like it grainy, it will take 15 to 20 minutes.

OVEN METHOD Preheat the oven to 350 degrees F. Butter a 13- by 8-inch shallow baking dish. In it combine the water, polenta, and salt. Cover with foil and bake for 15 minutes. Remove the foil and stir the polenta. Cover and continue baking another 15 or so minutes until all the water is absorbed.

COOK'S CHOICE POLENTA

Prepare the polenta as directed in the master recipe, following the Stove-top or Oven Method. When the polenta is cooked, stir in your choice of the following: 1 cup corn kernels; 1/4 cup chopped olives, pitted; 2 to 3 ounces goat cheese; 2 to 3 ounces cubed cheese; 1/2 cup olive salad; 1/2 cup sliced marinated artichoke hearts; 1 to 2 tablespoons herb blend; 1/2 cup sautéed sliced mushrooms; or 1/2 cup sautéed red and green bell peppers, seeded and chopped. Serve soft or pour polenta into a pan and let set until firm, 30 to 60 minutes, depending on thickness. If it is set, reheat in an oven preheated to 350 degrees F until heated through, about 20 minutes. Serve or reheat with a favorite pasta sauce.

POLENTA WITH SUN-DRIED TOMATOES AND BLUE CHEESE

Prepare the polenta as directed in the master recipe, following the Stove-top or Oven Method. When the polenta is cooked, stir in 2 tablespoons butter, 1/2 cup chopped sun-dried tomatoes, and 3 ounces (2/3 cup) blue cheese, crumbled. Serve immediately or pour into a pan to cool and set. When firm, slice and sauté, broil, or microwave to reheat.

STACKED POLENTA LOAF

Prepare the polenta as directed in the master recipe, following the Stove-top or Oven Method. When the polenta is cooked, stir in 2 tablespoons butter, then pour polenta into a loaf pan to set; it will take about 1 hour to firm up. Meanwhile, grate 4 to 5 ounces (1 cup) Monterey Jack or Cheddar cheese and have ready 3/4 cup olive salad and 1 cup pasta sauce. When the polenta has set, remove it from the pan and slice it lengthwise into thirds. Preheat oven to 350 degrees F. Butter the loaf pan and set one slice of polenta on the bottom. Cover with half the olive salad, half the grated cheese, and one-third of the sauce. Top with a slice of polenta, then repeat layers. Top with a third slice of polenta, and spoon on the last of the sauce. Bake until heated through, 25 to 30 minutes. Slice and serve with more sauce.

POLENTA TAMALE PIE

Before preparing the polenta, prepare one recipe Mexican Baked Beans (page 127). When the beans have cooked to serving point, pour them in an ovenproof or microwavable square or round casserole. Then, prepare the polenta as directed in the master recipe, following the Stove-top Method. When the polenta is cooked, stir in 2 to 3 tablespoons butter, 3 ounces ($\frac{1}{2}$ cup) grated Cheddar cheese, and $\frac{1}{4}$ cup chopped fresh parsley. Pour the polenta over the top of the beans and smooth the top. The dish can be made ahead to this point. Bake in an oven at 350 degrees F or microwave for about 20 to 30 minutes to heat through.

POLENTA PIZZA APPETIZERS

Prepare the polenta as directed in the master recipe (page 142). Pour polenta onto a rimmed baking sheet to a depth of $\frac{1}{4}$ inch and let cool. Cut out 18 to 20 rounds with a 3-inch cutter. (If you use commercial polenta rolls, these are made in minutes. A 1-pound, 8-ounce polenta roll makes two dozen $\frac{1}{4}$-inch-thick rounds.) Preheat the oven to 375 degrees F. Lay polenta rounds on a lightly oiled baking sheet. Brush them with $\frac{1}{4}$ cup garlic- or herb-infused oil. Set the baking sheet in the oven, turn on the broiler, and broil 3 to 4 minutes to crisp the edges of the polenta. Remove and turn each round over and brown the other side if desired. Turn off the broiler, but keep the oven on at 375 degrees F. Place a spoonful of pasta sauce (about 1 cup total) on each round and top with a little Italian salsa, caponata, or caramelized onion relish (about 1 cup total). Cut 3 ounces plain, pepper, or herb-flavored feta cheese into $\frac{1}{4}$-inch cubes and place one on each polenta round. Bake on the middle shelf until heated through, 10 to 15 minutes (feta holds its shape when hot so it won't appear melted). Serve hot.

PANTRY
TIPS

Grits and polenta are interchangeable. Their major difference is color – grits are white and polenta is yellow.

A polenta roll on hand in the refrigerator provides instant rounds for lunch, appetizers, and entrées.

PENNE WITH CAPONATA

Prepare the master recipe using penne noodles. In a medium saucepan, combine 1 1/2 cups caponata with 1 cup tomato sauce or pasta sauce. Add 1 teaspoon or so garlic paste, if you like. Pour over noodles and serve with grated Parmesan cheese and chopped fresh basil.

MUSHROOM FETTUCINE WITH MUSHROOM SAUCE

Prepare the master recipe using porcini or other mushroom-flecked fettucine. In a small saucepan, heat 2 cups (16 ounces) pasta sauce with mushrooms and pour over the pasta.

LEMON TAGLIARINI WITH SEAFOOD BROTH

Prepare the master recipe using lemon-flavored tagliarini. For the cooking water, substitute 3 cups fish, vegetable, or chicken stock (or broth). Stir in 1/2 teaspoon garlic paste, 1 tablespoon fish herb blend or fines herbes, and 1/2 cup dry white wine. Bring to a boil, add the pasta, and cook until tender, about 10 minutes. When the pasta is done, stir in 1/4 pound scallops and 1/4 pound medium shrimp, shelled and deveined. Divide the noodles and fish among four bowls and spoon the broth over them. Garnish with chopped fresh parsley and grated lemon zest.

CHINESE STIR-FRIED NOODLES

Prepare the master recipe using fresh or dried Chinese egg noodles and the following additions: In a skillet over medium heat warm 2 table-spoons safflower or canola oil. Sauté until softened, about 3 minutes, 4 green onions, sliced diagonally; 1 portobello or 4 shiitake mushrooms, sliced thinly; and 1/2 red bell pepper, seeded and thinly sliced. Add 1/2 to 3/4 cup stir-fry sauce or other favorite Chinese sauce and heat to serving temperature. Serve over the noodles, garnished with toasted sesame seeds or chopped green onion tops.

SZECHUAN SESAME NOODLES

Prepare the master recipe using fresh or dried Chinese egg noodles. In a bowl, combine 1/2 cup Szechuan sauce or Szechuan peanut sauce with 1 1/2 teaspoons garlic paste, 1 tablespoon rice vinegar, 1 tablespoon sesame oil, and 1 teaspoon hot chili oil (or to taste). While the pasta is cooking, spoon a few tablespoons of the cooking water into the sauce and stir to mix. When the pasta is done, toss with the sauce and garnish with minced fresh cilantro leaves and minced green onions. Sprinkle with toasted sesame seeds.

THAI PEANUT NOODLES

For this dish you will need two 3-ounce packages ramen noodles soaked in hot water for 15 minutes and drained. In a skillet over medium-high heat, warm 2 tablespoons of canola or safflower oil. Quickly stir-fry 3 garlic cloves, cut into slivers, and 4 shallots, cut into slivers. Drain them on paper towels and reserve. Add another tablespoon oil to the pan and sauté 1 carrot, grated, until just wilted. Stir in 1/2 to 2 teaspoons chile paste with garlic, 4 tablespoons tomato paste, 1 1/2 teaspoons sugar, and 2 tablespoons fish sauce. Stir in 1/2 cup chopped fresh basil. Add another 3 tablespoons oil and the noodles, stirring to mix with the sauce. Garnish with halved cherry tomatoes, chopped roasted peanuts, and the stir-fried garlic and shallot slivers.

PAD THAI

Prepare the master recipe using dried Asian noodles. In a skillet over medium heat, warm 2 tablespoons oil. Sauté 1 onion, chopped; 2 green onions, including tops, chopped; 1 green bell pepper, seeded and chopped; and 1 teaspoon garlic paste until soft. Stir in 1/4 to 1/2 cup dried peanut sauce mix plus one 14-ounce can (1 3/4 cups) coconut milk. Alternatively, stir in 2 cups peanut sauce, thinned with coconut milk if necessary. Bring to a boil and mix with the noodles. Garnish with chopped tomatoes, roasted peanuts, lime wedges, and chopped fresh cilantro or parsley.

ALBACORE PASTA SAUCE

Prepare the master recipe using spaghetti. Soak 1/4 pound dried mushrooms in warm water for 20 minutes. In a skillet over medium heat, warm 3 tablespoons olive oil. Sauté 1/2 onion, finely chopped; 1/2 red bell pepper, seeded and finely chopped; and 1 1/2 teaspoons garlic paste for 3 to 5 minutes. Stir in the mushrooms, drained, and one 28-ounce can (3 1/2 cups) crushed tomatoes in puree. Add salt and freshly ground black pepper to taste. Simmer the sauce 20 minutes or so to blend flavors. Add 1/3 to 1/2 pound fresh or canned albacore tuna, flaked into bite-sized pieces. Cook about 5 minutes for fresh albacore, just until heated through for canned albacore. Alternatively, the sauce can be made by heating a favorite pasta or marinara sauce, adding a little extra garlic and chopped fresh basil, and stirring in the albacore as directed.

CHINESE FRIED RICE

In a wok or nonstick skillet over medium heat, warm 2 tablespoons oil. Quickly scramble 1 beaten egg. Remove the egg and reserve. Then stir-fry $1/2$ onion, chopped, or 6 green onions, chopped, including the tops, for 1 minute. Add $1/2$ green bell pepper, seeded and chopped, and $1/2$ cup sliced mushrooms, and stir-fry until softened. Return the egg to the vegetables and add the cooked rice. Stir in $3/4$ cup stir-fry sauce and heat to serving temperature. Optional additions include cooked chicken or ham or pork, cooked broccoli, snow peas, squash, bean sprouts, or bamboo shoots.

SPANISH SKILLET RICE

Prepare the master recipe with these changes: When sautéing the onion, add $1/2$ green bell pepper, seeded and chopped, and 1 teaspoon garlic paste. Stir in 2 teaspoons dried oregano or marjoram or an herb blend. Add the rice and stir $3/4$ cup spicy tomato pasta sauce into the rice mixture. Heat to serving temperature as directed. Optional additions include $1/2$ pound browned ground beef or chorizo, or 1 to 2 sliced, sautéed sausages.

CURRIED SKILLET RICE

Prepare the master recipe with these changes and your choice of curry powder, paste, or sauce: When sautéing the onions, add 2 more cups chopped or sliced vegetables, such as squash, mushrooms, celery, bell peppers, broccoli, and eggplant, and cook until soft. If you are using curry paste, stir in $1/4$ cup paste mixed with $3/4$ cup coconut milk, stock, broth, or plain yogurt. If using curry powder, sauté 2 to 4 tablespoons of curry blend the last 30 seconds while sautéing the vegetables and then stir $3/4$ cup of coconut milk, stock, broth, or yogurt. If using curry sauce, simply stir $3/4$ to 1 cup into the rice and vegetables and heat to serving temperature as directed. Optional additions include $1/2$ pound cooked chicken or seafood, $1/2$ cup peas, and $1/2$ to 1 cup cooked garbanzo beans. Garnish with chopped fresh parsley or cilantro and sautéed sliced almonds, if desired.

SKILLET RICE MARINARA

Prepare the master recipe with these changes: When the onions are soft, stir in 1 teaspoon garlic paste and cook for 20 seconds. Also add 1/2 cup sliced mushrooms, if you like. Stir in the rice and use marinara or other highly seasoned pasta sauce for the liquid and heat to serving temperature. Garnish with chopped fresh basil and toasted pine nuts.

SZECHUAN FRIED RICE

Prepare the master recipe using white rice. For the sauce, use 1/3 cup Szechuan sauce and 1/4 cup stock or broth. Optional additions include minced chile paste, chopped peeled ginger, and 1 to 2 cups chopped vegetables.

PANTRY
TIPS

Leftover rice adds substance to soup, a stir-fry, or salad.

As a quick topping for pasta or rice, keep a variety of sauces such as curry and Szechuan in the pantry so you can create a meal in minutes.

For an easy Basque-style tuna sauce for pasta, combine 6 ounces drained albacore tuna with a favorite pasta sauce. Serve it over fettucine and garnish with chopped fresh basil or parsley. Pass the garlic bread.

BAKED RICE
serves 4 to 6

This is the easiest, no-fuss way to make great rice and a perfect showcase for international flavors. In the Middle East it is known as pilaf. Any way you choose to prepare it, baked rice is ready in less than an hour. Be sure to rinse the rice before baking to keep the grains separate.

2 cups long-grain white rice

1/2 to 1 teaspoon salt (depending on the saltiness of the other ingredients)

1 tablespoon butter

4 cups hot water, chicken or vegetable stock, or canned broth

Preheat the oven to 350 degrees F. Lightly oil or butter a 13- by 8-inch baking dish. Rinse the rice in a colander or strainer under running water to remove excess starch. Then combine the rice, salt, butter, and water in the baking dish. Cover with aluminum foil and bake 20 minutes. Remove from the oven, stir the rice, cover, and bake until the rice has absorbed all the liquid and the grains are tender, another 15 to 25 minutes. If you are using brown rice, increase the water to 4 1/2 cups and bake an additional 10 minutes. For wild rice, use 4 1/2 cups of water and bake an additional 20 minutes. If you use converted or instant rice, follow the directions for the amount of liquid on the package and bake as directed below; the time will be about 10 minutes.

FOR ONE PAN-SIZED CAKE In the skillet, over medium-high heat, warm the oil. Pour the rice mixture into the pan and spread it around with a spatula to make it an even thickness. Cook, shaking the pan periodically to free the bottom and sides of the cake, until set, about 5 minutes. Place a flat plate or cookie sheet on top of the pan, invert the skillet to free the rice cake from the pan, and slide it back into the skillet, browned side up. Continue cooking until the underside is set and browned, another 3 to 4 minutes. Invert it again onto a serving platter. Garnish with chopped fresh parsley and serve cut into wedges. Serves 3 to 4.

FOR SMALL CAKES In a well-seasoned cast-iron skillet or non-stick skillet over medium-high heat, warm the oil. Spoon the rice mixture onto the hot surface to form 3-inch cakes. Cook until set, 3 to 4 minutes. With a spatula turn the cakes over and continue cooking until lightly browned and set on the other side, 3 to 4 minutes longer. Continue until all the rice mixture is used. Garnish with parsley. Makes about twelve 3-inch cakes.

CREOLE RICE CAKE

Prepare the master recipe using white rice and these changes: Use an onion and, when sautéing it, add $1/2$ green bell pepper, seeded and chopped, and 1 tablespoon Creole or Cajun seasoning. Proceed as directed and serve with a Creole sauce or with barbecued shrimp.

CURRIED WILD RICE AND SALMON CAKE

Prepare the master recipe using wild rice and the following additions: Use green onions and when they are softened, stir in 1 or 2 table-spoons curry paste. Gently fold in 4 ounces cooked salmon. Proceed as directed.

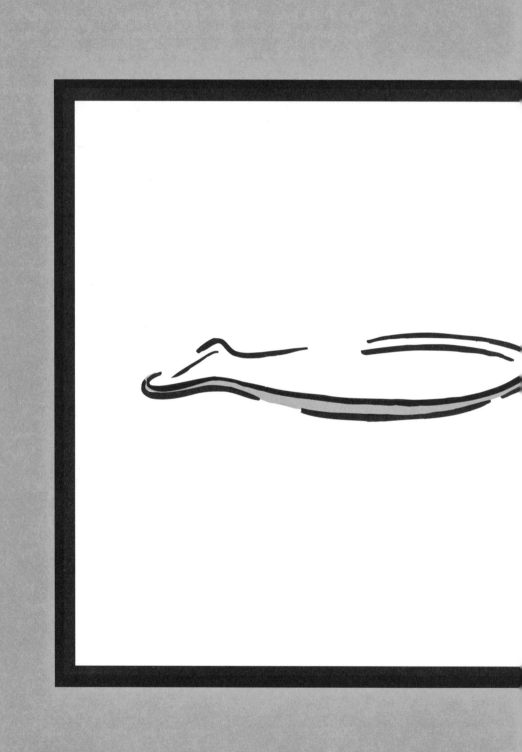

CHAPTER

fish + seafood

FIVE

Nothing does a heart better than a fresh-tasting morsel from the sea. Fortunately, flash-freezing and rapid transportation mean good **FISH** and **SEAFOOD** is available all over the country. I love the simplicity of a straightforward sautéed rockfish fillet, a broiled salmon steak, or grilled shrimp on skewers. The tempting array of condiments I've tried with them as accompaniments has brought much pleasure, and not a little excitement.

Here I share the basics — how to broil, bake, sauté, poach, and grill. The sauce is up to you. Rub the fish with a dry mix of spices, jerk seasoning, or a Cajun, barbecue, or herb blend. Marinate it in a citrus soak. Sauce it with a designated seafood sauce or teriyaki sauce. (If you have a finicky family, each fillet could be flavored differently at the same meal!)

When purchasing fillets of fish, make sure they are firm and smell fresh. Don't buy the ones at the bottom of the tray if they are sitting in the liquid that has drained off the fish all day. Their color should be bright and clear, not slimy or bruised. Some fillets still have their bones. Although pulling the little bones out of rockfish and salmon is easier after cooking, for special occasions I recommend a pair of tweezers to remove them before cooking. The basic rule for cooking a whole fish or fillet is 10 minutes per inch of thickness, measured at the thickest part.

**Sautéed
Fish Fillets**
page 166

Broiled Fillets
page 170

**Baked
Fish Fillets**
page 172

RECIPE
LIST

**Grilled Whole Fish
and Fillets**
page 186

Fish Cakes
page 174

Seafood Boil
page 184

Fish Stew
page 176

Shrimp
page 180

SAUTÉED FISH FILLETS

serves 4

Sautéing offers a one-skillet way to get fish immediately on the table. It also marries the flavors of the sauce with the cooking before you serve it. Try a flavored oil for the initial sautéing. Then remove the fillets, keeping them warm, and deglaze the pan with your sauce of choice. Just pour the sauce into the hot pan and scrape up the bits of cooked food stuck to the pan bottom and mix with the sauce. Most fillets are a half-inch thick or less, so don't overcook. If you first put fillets in the pan skinned side up, they look prettier for serving when flipped over.

4 fillets of fish, 4 to 5 ounces each; or 1 large fillet, 1 1/2 pounds, cut into 4 serving pieces

2 tablespoons all-purpose flour

2 tablespoons oil

Salt and ground black or white pepper

1 cup sauce

Dredge the fish in the flour and set on a plate. In a skillet large enough to hold all the fillets in one layer, warm the oil over medium-high heat. When the oil is hot, carefully slide in the fish, skinned-side up. Cook for 2 to 4 minutes on one side, turn them over with a spatula, and cook until done, 2 to 4 minutes. Test for doneness by pressing into the thickest part. If your finger leaves a dent, the fillet is rare in the middle. Cook until it springs back when pressed; but just to that point. Don't overcook. Season with salt and pepper and deglaze the pan with a sauce (see above) and serve over the fish.

SEASONED FISH SAUTÉ

Up to one hour ahead, rub 1 to 2 teaspoons dry herb, spice blend, or paste over both sides of each fillet. Omit the sauce. When ready to cook, proceed as directed in the master recipe.

BLACKENED FISH

Prepare the master recipe using redfish or snapper fillets and these changes: Just before cooking, rub a total of 1 to 2 teaspoons of Cajun blackened-fish spices over the fillets in place of the flour. For the most authentic results, heat a cast-iron skillet with the 2 tablespoons of oil until almost smoking. Carefully slide in the fish and sauté 2 to 3 minutes on each side.

SAUTÉED FISH WITH SIMPLE PAN SAUCE

Prepare the master recipe as directed, then remove the fillets from the pan and keep them warm. To make a pan sauce, pour off any fat in the skillet, then deglaze the pan by adding in 1 cup sauce, or $1/2$ cup vinegar, verjus, or marinade and let it sizzle over high heat. Scrape up any crusty bits of food from the pan bottom and mix with the sauce. Boil if necessary to reduce and thicken the sauce, or simply heat to serving temperature. Pour over the fish and serve.

MARINATED FISH SAUTÉ

Up to 1 hour ahead, place the fillets in a ceramic or glass dish and cover with $1/2$ to $3/4$ cup marinade or teriyaki sauce. When ready to cook, remove the fillets from the marinade and proceed as directed in the master recipe. You may deglaze the pan with the marinade to make a pan sauce, if you like.

SAUCY FILLETS

Prepare the master recipe with these changes: When the pan and oil are hot, quickly brown the fillets on both sides. Then pour in 1 cup or more of sauce (the amount depends on whether you want to serve the fish and sauce over something else such as rice, pasta, potatoes, or polenta). Finish cooking the fillets in the sauce. Optionally, the fish can be cut into bite-sized pieces, browned, and finished in the sauce to serve over rice, pasta, potatoes, or polenta.

CARIBBEAN FISH SAUTÉ

Up to 1 hour ahead, rub 1 teaspoon (or to taste) jerk seasoning over both sides of each fillet. Prepare the master recipe as directed, then remove the fillets from the pan and keep them warm. To make a pan sauce, pour off any grease in the skillet, then deglaze the pan by adding 1 1/2 cups coconut milk. Scrape up any crusty bits of food from the bottom and mix with sauce. Boil for 3 to 4 minutes to reduce and thicken the sauce. Pour over the fish and garnish with lime wedges. The coconut milk is a refreshing counterpoint to the spicy jerked fish.

SAUTÉED FISH WITH BLACK BEAN SAUCE

Prepare the master recipe as directed, then remove the fillets from the pan, and keep warm. To make a pan sauce, pour off any fat in the skillet, then deglaze the pan by adding 3 to 4 tablespoons bean sauce (or 2 tablespoons fermented black beans plus 1 tablespoon fish sauce), 1 tablespoon tomato paste, and 1/2 cup stock, broth, wine, or water and let the liquid sizzle over high heat. Scrape up any crusty bits of food from the bottom and mix with the sauce. If using the prepared sauce, cook to heat through and serve over the fish fillets. If using black beans and fish sauce, boil 2 to 3 minutes to blend flavors. Pour over the fish and garnish with lime wedges.

PANTRY
TIP

For an Asian seafood marinade, combine 1/4 cup soy sauce or tamari, 1 teaspoon garlic paste, 2 whole green onions, finely chopped, 1 to 2 tablespoons mirin, and 1 to 2 tablespoons rice wine (or sherry) vinegar.

BROILED FILLETS

serves 4

Although you can broil fish completely free of added fat, brushing fillets with a little oil, especially one infused with lemon or roasted garlic, adds more flavor and a slight gloss to the fish. Coating the fish before cooking with an herb or spice blend adds that much more flavor.

4 fish fillets, 4 to 5 ounces each, or 1 large fillet, 1 1/2 pounds

2 to 3 tablespoons safflower or canola oil or any flavored oil

1 tablespoon herb or spice blend (optional)

Preheat the broiler to 425 degrees F. Brush the fish with oil, coat with seasoning (if using), and place on a broiling pan. Place the fish 4 inches from the heat. Broil individual fillets, skinned side up first, for 3 to 4 minutes on each side. If you are broiling a whole fillet, leave it on for 3 to 4 minutes longer. To test for doneness, gently press in the flesh with your finger, it will feel firm and spring back if it is cooked through.

BROILED SEASONED FISH

For a spicy Cajun, barbecue, fajita, curry, or Caribbean flavor, up to 1 hour ahead, combine 2 tablespoons dry spice or herb blend or rub with 2 tablespoons flour and dredge the fillets in this mixture. When ready to cook, proceed as directed in the master recipe.

MARINATED BROILED FISH

Up to 2 hours ahead, place the fillets in a ceramic or glass dish and cover with $1/2$ to $3/4$ cup teriyaki sauce, barbecue sauce, or other marinade. When ready to cook, remove the fillets from the marinade and proceed as directed in the master recipe.

BROILED FISH WITH SIMPLE PAN SAUCE

Prepare the master recipe as directed, then remove the fillets from the pan, and keep them warm. To make a pan sauce, deglaze the pan by adding $1/2$ to $3/4$ cup marinade or sauce into the hot broiler pan and let it sizzle. Scrape up any bits of food from the pan bottom and mix with the sauce. Pour the sauce into a saucepan and boil for a minute or so to heat it well and incorporate the pan juices. Pour over fish and serve.

SOUTH-OF-THE-BORDER BROILED FISH

Prepare the master recipe with the following additions: In a plate combine 1 teaspoon achiote paste with $1/4$ cup water or white wine. Dip the fillets in this mixture, then cook as directed; remove the fillets from the pan and keep them warm. To make a pan sauce, deglaze the pan by adding $1/2$ cup salsa to the hot broiler pan and let it sizzle. Scrape up any bits of food from the pan bottom and mix with the sauce. Pour the sauce into the saucepan and boil for a minute or so to heat it well and incorporate the pan juices. Pour over fish and serve.

BAKED
FISH FILLETS
serves 4

Depending on the marinade or sauce you choose, baking can be a fat-free way to cook fish. If you cook the fish in a ceramic or heat-resistant glass baking dish, reduce the temperature by 25 degrees F and add 8 to 10 minutes to the cooking time to give the glass time to heat up.

4 fish fillets, 4 to 5 ounces each, or 1 large fillet, 1 1/2 pounds

2 tablespoons dry rub, herb or spice blend, or paste

Salt and ground black or white pepper

Preheat the oven to 375 degrees F. Lightly oil a baking pan. (If you use a heat-resistant glass baking dish, lower the heat to 350 degrees F.) Season the fillets on both sides with the herbs or spices and salt and pepper, then lay them in the pan. Bake until the fish is firm and cooked through, 12 to 15 minutes for individual fillets, 16 to 20 minutes for a large fillet.

MARINATED BAKED FISH

Up to 2 hours ahead, place the fillets in a ceramic or glass dish and cover with $1/2$ to $3/4$ cup teriyaki sauce, barbecue sauce, or other marinade. When ready to cook, remove the fillets from the marinade and proceed as directed in the master recipe.

BAKED FISH WITH SIMPLE PAN SAUCE

Prepare the master recipe as directed, then remove the fillets from the pan and keep them warm. To make a pan sauce, deglaze the dish by adding $3/4$ cup of marinade or sauce into the hot baking dish and letting it sizzle. Scrape up any bits of food from the bottom of the dish and mix with the sauce. Pour the sauce into a saucepan and boil for a minute or so to heat it well and incorporate the pan juices.

OVEN-POACHED FILLET

Prepare the master recipe, adding $3/4$ to 1 cup white wine, stock, stewed tomatoes, or other sauce to the pan. Increase the baking time by about 4 minutes.

PANTRY
TIPS

Make Wasabi Red Pepper Sauce for any fish, or as a topping for canapés when mixed with cooked bay shrimp or crab. This recipe is adapted from one shared by John Carles. Combine $1/2$ cup red pepper spread with 2 to 3 teaspoons wasabi, 2 to 3 teaspoons red wine vinegar, and $1/2$ cup mayonnaise.

Brush lemon-infused oil over fillets of fish before grilling or broiling for a pleasant citrus accent.

FISH CAKES

serves 4

When the budget allows for only a small amount of fish, or when unexpected guests drop by and the fish has already been purchased, fish cakes are the answer. Combine expensive seafood such as scallops, lobster, shrimp, and/or crab meat with less expensive rockfish to add a wonderful richness to the cakes. Shrimp also impart their pink color and firm texture, two good reasons for including them. Remove all shells and chop seafood to make a workable mixture.

1 pound fish fillets, finely chopped, or other seafood, finely or coarsely chopped

3 green onions, including green tops, finely chopped

1 egg

1/2 to 3/4 cup dried bread crumbs

Salt and ground black or white pepper

1/2 red and/or green bell pepper, seeded and chopped (optional)

2 tablespoons canola or safflower oil

In a mixing bowl, combine seafood with green onions, egg, bread crumbs, salt and pepper to taste and bell pepper (if using). Form into 4 patties. In a skillet over medium-high heat warm the oil. Fry the cakes, turning once, cooking until golden brown and cooked through, 3 to 4 minutes on each side.

THAI CURRIED FISH CAKES

Prepare the master recipe and stir in 1 tablespoon red, green, or yellow Thai curry paste or spice blend. Add ¼ cup coconut milk and 1 teaspoon fish sauce and mix to blend all. Form into patties and cook as directed.

MEDITERRANEAN FISH CAKES

Prepare the master recipe and stir in ½ teaspoon garlic paste, the red bell pepper, and 1 tablespoon Mediterranean or other herb blend. Form into patties and cook as directed. Serve with aioli (see page 121).

WASABI-RED PEPPER FISH CAKES

Prepare the master recipe and stir in ¼ teaspoon wasabi paste, ½ teaspoon garlic paste, and 1 to 2 teaspoons soy sauce. Form into patties and cook as directed. Serve with Wasabi Red Pepper Sauce (see page 173).

MEXICAN FISH CAKES

Prepare the master recipe and stir in ½ teaspoon garlic paste, 2 to 3 teaspoons Mexican herb blend, and ¼ cup chopped fresh cilantro. Form into patties and cook as directed. Serve with salsa.

CURRY-CHUTNEY FISH CAKES

Prepare the master recipe and stir in 1 to 2 teaspoons curry paste and ¼ cup coconut milk (optional). Form into patties and cook as directed. Serve with chutney topping: Heat in a small saucepan ½ cup chutney, 2 whole minced green onions, ½ teaspoon garlic paste, and ¼ cup fresh lime juice. Bring to a boil, cool, and serve.

AIOLI-TOPPED FISH CAKES

Prepare the master recipe, using red and green bell peppers. Top with aioli (see page 121).

FISH STEW

serves 4 to 6

Fish stews are all-season dishes, depending on the lightness of the broth and the heaviness of the vegetables. Also see Fish Soup (page 86).

2 tablespoons canola, safflower, or olive oil

1 onion, sliced or chopped

1 to 3 garlic cloves, minced, or $1/2$ to $11/2$ teaspoons garlic paste

$1/2$ cup white or red wine

2 cups stock, tomato sauce, or water

1 to 2 tablespoons herb blend

Salt and ground black or white pepper

$13/4$ pounds seafood, such as fish fillets, cut in 1-inch pieces; shrimp, shelled and deveined; crab meat; lobster; and/or squid, cut into rings

2 to 3 pounds mussels and/or clams (optional)

$1/2$ cup white wine or water (optional)

Chopped fresh parsley, for garnish

In a deep skillet over medium-high heat, warm the oil. Sauté the onion until soft, 2 to 3 minutes. Add the garlic and sauté another 20 seconds. Stir in $1/2$ cup red or white wine, the stock, herbs, and salt and pepper to taste. Bring to a boil, reduce heat to medium, and simmer to blend flavors, about 10 minutes. You can prepare the recipe to this point up to 1 day in advance.

(continued at right)

Ten minutes before serving, bring the broth to a simmer if made ahead, drop in the seafood, and cook just until all is done, 3 to 5 minutes. If using mussels and/or clams, cook them while the other seafood simmers in the broth. Place them in a shallow pan with 1/2 cup white wine and cook, covered, until the shells open and they are firm, 5 to 8 minutes. Spoon them on top of the stew. Sprinkle with chopped fresh parsley and serve hot.

MEDITERRANEAN FISH STEW

Prepare the master recipe with these changes: Sauté 1/2 green bell pepper, seeded and sliced, with the onion. Add the larger amount of garlic. For the 2 cups liquid, along with the wine, use herb pasta sauce or marinara sauce. Omit the herb blend.

MEXICAN FISH STEW

Prepare the master recipe with these changes: Sauté 1/2 green bell pepper, seeded and sliced, with the onion. For the liquid, substitute salsa for the 1/2 cup red or white wine, and use 2 cups enchilada, red chile, or other spicy tomato sauce. Use a Mexican herb blend.

GUMBO

Prepare the master recipe with these changes: Sauté 1/2 green bell pepper, seeded and sliced, and 1 celery stalk, chopped, with the onion. Sprinkle 2 tablespoons all-purpose flour over the cooked vegetables and sauté 2 to 3 minutes to cook the flour. For the liquid, omit the 1/2 cup red or white wine and use 2 1/2 cups stewed or chopped tomatoes. Use a Cajun or Creole herb blend. In addition, stir in gumbo's signature ingredient – 1/2 cup whole or sliced fresh or frozen okra. Just after adding the fish, reduce heat to medium and stir in 1 tablespoon filé powder (don't boil, or the filé could become stringy). Optional additions include sliced cooked sausage or cubes of ham.

NEW ENGLAND FISH STEW

Prepare the master recipe with these changes: Sprinkle 2 tablespoons all-purpose flour over the sautéed onions and garlic and sauté 2 to 3 minutes to cook flour. For the liquid, use 1 cup stock or water and 1 cup milk. Use any favorite herb blend. Add 1 1/2 cups cooked, cubed potatoes to the liquid. Add the fish and cook as directed.

JAPANESE FISH STEW

Prepare the master recipe with these changes: For the liquid, use 2 1/2 cups fish stock or water and omit the 1/2 cup red or white wine. Omit the herb blend. When the liquid comes to a boil, stir in 1/4 pound dried soba (buckwheat) noodles, broken into 2-inch pieces. When the noodles are tender, add the fish and cook as directed.

SOUTH AMERICAN FISH STEW

Before preparing the master recipe, dissolve 1/2 teaspoon achiote paste in 1/4 cup water. Brush or rub the mixture on the seafood up to 2 hours before cooking. For the liquid, use 1 1/2 cups of crushed tomatoes in puree and 1/2 cup stock or water. Omit the wine and the herb blend. Optionally, add 1 cup cooked cubed or sliced potatoes and 1 cup corn kernels. Add the seafood and cook as directed. Garnish with chopped avocado and lime wedges.

PANTRY
EQUIVALENTS

SEAFOOD

4 to 5 ounces fish fillet equals 1 entrée serving

A 1$\frac{1}{2}$-pound whole fish equals 2 to 4 entrée servings

1 pound raw shrimp in their shells equals 3 entrée servings; 4 to 6 servings in
stews, paella, jambalaya, or other combined dishes

1$\frac{1}{2}$ to 2 pounds mussels or clams in their shells equals 1 entrée serving;
4 to 6 servings in stews, paella, jambalaya, or other seafood mixtures

2 teaspoons herb or spice blend or paste will coat a
4- to 5-ounce fish fillet (use less or to taste if the blend is heavy on chiles;
thin it with flour if you like)

$\frac{1}{2}$ cup sauce will deglaze a fish sauté pan; use the lesser
amount to glaze the fish, more if the sautéed fish and pan sauces
will top pasta, rice, or polenta

CITRUS

1 lime equals 1 to 2 tablespoons of fresh juice

1 lemon equals 2 to 4 tablespoons of fresh juice

SHRIMP

serves 4 to 6

Shrimp is one of my favorite bases for trying out the most pungent sauces such as curry, Szechuan, and black bean. Its texture holds up to strong flavors, whether cooked in the sauce or served with a dip. Cook shrimp just until they turn pink (overcooking makes them tough). Here are four basic methods to prepare tender, tasty shrimp.

2 to 4 tablespoons herb or spice blend

Salt and ground black or white pepper

1½ pounds medium shrimp, shelled and deveined

2 tablespoons plain or flavored oil (if grilling or sautéing)

Teriyaki, curry, marinara, or other sauce (optional for baking)

TO SAUTÉ Season the shrimp. Heat 2 tablespoons oil in a skillet and sauté shrimp just until pink, 2 to 4 minutes, depending on the size.

TO BROIL Preheat the broiler. Season the shrimp and either skewer them or have tongs ready to turn them over. Place them on a pan and broil, turning once, just until pink, 4 minutes total.

TO BAKE Preheat the oven to 425 degrees F. Season the shrimp. Combine the shrimp with ¾ to 1½ cups teriyaki, curry, marinara, or other sauce, if desired. Bake without sauce, 5 to 7 minutes; with sauce, 10 to 15 minutes.

TO GRILL Prepare the barbecue. Season the shrimp, brush with 2 tablespoons plain or flavored oil, and thread on bamboo skewers that have been soaked in water 15 to 20 minutes. Grill over hot coals, turning once, 3 to 5 minutes.

DRY-SEASONED SHRIMP

Up to 1 hour before preparing master recipe, rub the shrimp in 1 or 2 teaspoons of a dry herb or spice blend. Sauté, broil, bake, or grill as directed in the master recipe.

MARINATED SHRIMP

Up to 1 hour ahead, place the shrimp in a ceramic or glass dish and cover with $1/2$ to $3/4$ cup teriyaki sauce or other marinade. When ready to cook, remove the shrimp from the marinade and bake, broil, grill, or sauté as directed in the master recipe. You can make a pan sauce with the marinade by pouring it into the hot pan used to cook the shrimp (grilling excepted). Scrape up any crusty bits of food from the pan bottom and mix with the sauce. Pour the sauce in a saucepan and boil for 2 to 3 minutes.

GRILLED SMOKY SHRIMP (OR SCALLOPS)

Plan on 4 or 5 medium shrimp or 3 or 4 large prawns, all shelled and deveined, per person (or 5 or 6 sea scallops). Coat each portion with 2 teaspoons dry barbecue rub or seasoning, or 2 tablespoons of marinade. To ease their maneuvering on the grill, thread each portion on skewers (if using bamboo, soak them in water for 15 to 20 minutes before skewering). Grill as directed in the master recipe.

BAKED GREEK SHRIMP

In a baking dish, combine the shrimp with $1/2$ cup wine, $1/2$ cup stewed tomatoes or tomato pasta sauce, and 8 or more Greek olives, pitted and halved. Sprinkle with 4 ounces feta cheese, crumbled or cubed. Bake as directed in the master recipe with a sauce.

SPICY TOMATO SHRIMP

In a skillet over medium-high heat, warm 2 tablespoons oil. Sauté the shrimp just until pink. Stir in $1/2$ teaspoon garlic paste and sauté 30 seconds longer. Stir in 2 cups spicy pasta sauce or 2 cups crushed tomatoes in puree, combined with 2 to 4 tablespoons of red pepper relish and $1/2$ to 2 teaspoons chile paste (to taste). Bring to a boil, remove from heat, and serve over pasta or rice. To bake the shrimp, combine the shrimp, garlic, and sauce ingredients in a shallow baking dish, and bake as directed in the master recipe with a sauce.

THAI CURRIED SHRIMP

In a skillet over high heat, warm 2 tablespoons oil. Quickly sear the shrimp on both sides and remove. Stir in 1 teaspoon garlic paste and 1 onion, chopped, and sauté until onion is softened. Add 2 to 4 table-spoons Thai red, yellow, or green curry spice mixture and $1 1/2$ cups coconut milk. Stir in 1 to 2 teaspoons fish sauce and bring to a boil. Return the shrimp to the pan and cook another 3 to 5 minutes. Serve garnished with chopped roasted peanuts and lime wedges.

GINGER-GARLIC TERIYAKI SHRIMP

In a skillet over high heat, warm 2 tablespoons oil. Quickly sear the shrimp on both sides and remove. Stir in 1 teaspoon garlic paste and 1 teaspoon minced peeled ginger. Let sizzle for about 20 seconds and add $1/2$ cup teriyaki sauce and $1/4$ cup stock. Cook to reduce slightly, 3 to 5 minutes. Return the shrimp to the pan and cook until shrimp is glazed with sauce. Serve over rice, garnished with toasted sesame seeds.

SWEET-AND-SOUR SHRIMP

In a skillet over high heat, warm 2 tablespoons oil. Sauté $1/2$ green bell pepper, seeded and sliced; $1/2$ onion, sliced; and 1 teaspoon garlic paste. Stir in 1 pound shrimp, shelled and deveined, and cook just until pink. Then, stir in $1 1/2$ cups sweet-and-sour sauce (thin with stock or water if necessary) and bring just to a boil. Add 1 cup blanched broc-coli florets and serve over rice. Serves 4.

SEAFOOD BOIL

serves 6 to 8

Best done on the beach (but also easily accomplished on top of the stove), a seafood boil is personalized by various regional styles and the local catch. The concept involves getting the freshest fish and shellfish and cooking it simply with a big pot of vegetables and seasoning. The master recipe reflects the style of the Low Country around the Sea Islands off the coast of South Carolina and Georgia.

2 to 3 gallons water

3 to 4 tablespoons seafood boil seasoning blend

2 onions, chopped or quartered

2 green bell peppers, seeded and chopped or quartered (optional)

2 celery stalks, chopped or quartered

4 to 6 new potatoes, peeled or unpeeled, quartered or whole

Optional vegetables: green beans; carrot sticks; corn on the cob, cut in half; whole okra; zucchini spears

Salt and freshly ground black pepper

2 to 4 pounds assorted shellfish such as whole or sectioned crab; shrimp; and clams, scallops, and mussels in their shells, in any combination

In a large pot bring the water to boil and add the seasoning blend. Stir in the vegetables and salt and pepper to taste. Cook until the vegetables are tender, 10 to 20 minutes. Stir in the seafood, and cook until done, another 10 minutes or so. With a slotted spoon, retrieve the ingredients and place in bowls, then ladle broth over them, or serve broth separately.

LOW COUNTRY SEAFOOD BOIL

Use a Low Country seasoning mix, but as some are quite salty, adjust the salt accordingly. Prepare the master recipe with green peppers, corn, and okra. Use shrimp and crab for the seafood.

CAJUN CRAWFISH BOIL

Omit the onions, peppers, and all the vegetables called for in the master recipe except small whole new potatoes, unpeeled. Bring the water to boil, stir in 2 to 3 tablespoons crawfish boil seasoning, and boil 5 minutes. Then add 12 to 18 small new potatoes. When the new potatoes are almost cooked, about 15 minutes, stir in 12 to 20 pounds of crawfish (the amount varies depending on how much the diners love crawfish!). Cook until the crawfish are bright red and firm to the touch, 15 to 20 minutes. Retrieve the potatoes and crawfish from the pot and place in bowls, then ladle broth over them, or serve separately. To eat the crawfish, twist off the head and discard. Pinch the very end of the tail to separate the meat from the shell, raise the tail to your lips, and suck out the delicious lobsterlike morsel.

WATERZOOI

This Flemish dish, whose name means cooking water, is distinguished by using a classic fines herbes blend (bay leaf, thyme, and parsley). Prepare the master recipe using only 8 cups of stock or water for the liquid and include perch, eel, or pike in the pot.

GRILLED WHOLE FISH
and FILLETS
serves 4

Albacore, salmon, sea bass, halibut, and rockfish lend themselves to grilling with the aplomb of a canvas waiting for color. Go easy on sauces and seasonings for seafood, since the texture and flavor of each fish or shellfish should be accented and enhanced, not overwhelmed. As always, taste the product you are about to use before marinating or brushing it on the ingredient.

1 large fish fillet, $1/2$ **pound, or 4 small fish fillets, 4 to 5 ounces each**

$1/4$ **cup dry seasoning rub** or $1/2$ cup marinade

Up to 1 hour ahead, rub the fillet with the seasoning or brush with marinade and refrigerate. About 30 minutes ahead, prepare the barbecue, preferably with mesquite or alderwood, until coals are red-hot and glowing. Oil the grill and place the fish on it, skinned side up. Grill 2 minutes on each side, then move the fish so it is next to, not over, the coals. Finish cooking until the fish is firm to the touch but not falling apart, 5 to 8 minutes longer. Serve with a sauce, if you like.

GRILLED PESTO SALMON

Prepare the master recipe using a 3- or 4-pound salmon fillet (with the skin). For the marinade, combine 1/4 cup basil-flavored oil, the juice of 2 limes, and salt and freshly ground black pepper to taste. Up to 5 hours ahead, brush the salmon with marinade. Wrap the fillet in aluminum foil and refrigerate until just before cooking. About 30 minutes ahead, prepare the barbecue, preferably with mesquite or alderwood, until coals are red-hot and glowing. Oil the grill, unwrap the salmon, and place it, skin side down, on the grill, next to, not over, the coals. Grill, covered, until the salmon is just oozing white juices and almost firm to the touch, 10 to 15 minutes. Serves 6 to 8.

GRILLED BASQUE TUNA

Prepare the master recipe using a 3- or 4-pound albacore or other tuna fillet, skinned. For the marinade, combine 1/2 cup pasta sauce with 1/4 cup white wine. Stir in 1 or 2 teaspoons fines herbes or other herb blend as you like. Up to 4 hours ahead, place the fillet in a ceramic or glass dish and pour the marinade over it. Cover and refrigerate until just before cooking. About 30 minutes ahead, prepare the barbecue, preferably with mesquite or alderwood, until coals are red-hot and glowing. Oil the grill, and cook the fillet over the coals, skinned side up, about 5 minutes. Turn over and place the fish next to, not over, the coals. Grill, covered, until the fish is cooked and slightly firm to the touch, 10 to 15 minutes (depending on thickness of fillet). Serve with a hot sauce made with additional pasta sauce mixed with wine. Serves 6 to 8.

GRILLED TERIYAKI ROCKFISH

Prepare the master recipe using four 5-ounce rockfish fillets or a 1 1/2-pound fillet. About 30 minutes ahead, brush the fish on both sides with 1/2 cup teriyaki sauce and prepare the barbecue as directed in the master recipe. When the coals are ready, brush the fish again with the sauce and cook as directed in the master recipe, brushing occasionally with more sauce to give the fish a shiny finish. Teriyaki has a tendency to caramelize, so adjust the exposure of the fish accordingly to the heat of the coals so it doesn't burn.

poultry +

meat

A tender piece of beef, a distinctive bite of pork, a cube of lamb, or a juicy morsel of chicken are transformed from day to day by reaching into the pantry. While pasta and other grains cool hot curries and Mexican moles, **MEAT** and **POULTRY** soak in the chiles, aromatics, and spices and convey their full potential with each tantalizing forkful. Take a trip to Bombay, Guadalajara, Kingston, Bangkok, Marrakech, or Naples, changing the destination daily by the seasoning and sauce options at your fingertips.

Chicken Sauté

page 192

Roast Chicken

page 196

**Chicken and Meat
on the Grill**

page 216

**Turkey or Chicken
Breast Escallops
Sauté**

page 198

RECIPE
LIST

Fajitas

page 214

Chicken Stew

page 200

Curry

page 210

Meat Stew

page 206

**Seasoned Meat
Loaf or Patties**

page 204

CHICKEN SAUTÉ

serves 4

With a sauté, you can have chicken every night and it never tastes the same. I start the chicken in a skillet and finish it in a baking dish in the oven. It can, however, be completely made on top of the stove by covering the skillet and stirring the mixture occasionally to keep it from sticking. Skinning the chicken reduces the amount of fat, yet it still stays moist and tender cooked this way. A sprinkle of paprika speeds browning.

2 tablespoons safflower, canola, or olive oil

1 chicken, 3 to 4 pounds, cut into serving pieces and skinned, or 3 to 4 pounds favorite chicken parts

Salt and freshly ground black pepper

3 to 4 garlic cloves, quartered or minced, or 2 teaspoons garlic paste

1 cup wine, stock, broth, or water

Preheat the oven to 350 degrees F. In skillet over high heat, warm the oil. Brown the chicken, a few pieces at a time, until well colored. Remove chicken to a baking dish and season with salt and pepper. To make a pan sauce, pour off any fat in the skillet, stir in the garlic, then deglaze the pan by adding the wine and let it sizzle over high heat. Scrape up any crusty bits of food from pan bottom and stir into the wine sauce. Boil for about 1 minute. Pour the pan sauce over the chicken, cover with foil, and bake 20 minutes. Remove the foil and continue baking until the chicken is cooked through, 5 to 10 minutes longer. Serve with rice, polenta, or pasta.

MEDITERRANEAN CHICKEN SAUTÉ

Prepare the master recipe with these changes: Sauté 3 or 4 garlic cloves, halved (or add 1 to 2 teaspoons garlic paste with the liquid), with the chicken. For the liquid, combine 1 cup marinara or other pasta sauce and 1 to 1 1/2 cups white wine. Optional additions include 1 to 2 tablespoons pesto, 1/4 cup chopped green olives, or chopped fresh parsley or basil. Cook as directed. Serve with pasta.

INDIAN CHICKEN SAUTÉ

Prepare the master recipe using 1 1/2 cups prepared curry sauce for the liquid (taste to see if you like the heat; add stock, broth, or water to dilute, if necessary). Serve with rice.

MEXICAN CHICKEN SAUTÉ

Prepare the master recipe using 1 cup fajita sauce or 2 tablespoons fajita or other Mexican seasoning combined with 1 1/2 cups tomato, enchilada, or other Mexican sauce for the liquid. Serve with rice.

CHINESE SWEET-AND-SOUR CHICKEN SAUTÉ

Prepare the master recipe using 1 cup sweet-and-sour sauce for the liquid. Optional additions include 2 tablespoons oil added to the pan after the fat is poured off in which to sauté until soft 1/2 onion, sliced, and 1/2 green bell pepper, seeded and sliced. Then, stir in the sweet-and-sour sauce and continue as directed in the master recipe. Before serving, stir in 1/2 cup cubed fresh or canned pineapple, if desired. Serve with rice.

ITALIAN OLIVE CHICKEN SAUTÉ

Instead of chicken, you could also try duck here. Prepare the master recipe with these changes: Use 2 cups red wine for the liquid, plus 2 to 4 tablespoons tapenade and 1 to 2 tablespoons tomato paste. Cook as directed, then pour off the pan sauce into a saucepan. Boil over high heat until the sauce is reduced to a thick coating. Pour over chicken and serve with pasta or polenta.

SAUTÉED CHICKEN WITH CHINESE BLACK BEAN SAUCE

Prepare the master recipe with these changes: For the liquid, use 2 to 3 tablespoons black bean sauce and 1 cup of stock, broth, or water. Alternatively, use 2 tablespoons mashed salted black beans; 2 teaspoons chopped peeled ginger; 1/2 cup rice wine; 2 tablespoons mirin; and 1 cup of stock, broth, or water. Dissolve 2 tablespoons cornstarch in 2 tablespoons water. Cook as directed, then pour off the pan sauce into a saucepan. Over medium heat, stir in the cornstarch mixture and bring to a boil to thicken. Coat chicken with sauce and serve with rice.

SAUTÉED CHICKEN WITH BARBECUE SAUCE

Prepare the master recipe using 1 cup favorite barbecue sauce for the liquid. Serve with potato salad.

KUNG PAO CHICKEN SAUTÉ

Prepare the master recipe with these changes: After the chicken is browned, sauté until softened 1/2 green bell pepper, seeded and sliced, and 1/2 onion, sliced. Stir in 1 cup kung pao sauce (dilute to taste with stock, broth, or water), a drop of toasted sesame oil, and hot oil to taste. Finish cooking as directed. Serve with rice.

PANTRY
TIPS

To cool your lips from burning spices on chicken or meat, melt ricotta or soft goat cheese over the meat before taking it off the burner or grill.

Make a cross-cultural glaze for grilled or roasted meats by combining 1/4 cup soy sauce with 2 tablespoons Dijon-style or orange- or ginger-flavored mustard.

ROAST CHICKEN

serves 4 to 6

This basic recipe for roasted chicken has lively suggestions for coating the chicken with distinctive ethnic flavors. I prefer roasting a whole chicken on a vertical roasting rack, which creates the most beautiful, even-colored bronze skin. If the sauce is too thin and slides off the skin of a chicken roasted vertically, roast the chicken on its back. Some sauces, such as teriyaki and barbecue, have sugar in them and tend to burn quickly. To prevent this, cover the bird with foil after the chicken starts to brown. To check for doneness, wiggle the drumstick and thigh. Both will move easily when fully cooked. Another test is to prick next to the thigh. If the juices run clear, thechicken is done.

1 chicken, 3^1/$_2$ to 4 pounds, whole or cut into serving pieces (skinned, if desired)

^{1}/$_4$ **to 1 cup glaze or sauce** or 2 tablespoons herb or spice mixture mixed with ^{1}/$_4$ cup olive oil

Preheat the oven to 350 degrees F. Wash chicken and pat dry with paper towels. Coat whole chicken or chicken parts with a glaze or sauce (a cut-up chicken will take up to 1 cup of sauce) or herbs. Place whole chicken on a vertical roaster in a roasting pan (add ^{1}/$_2$ cup water or stock to the pan) or set on its back on a lightly greased rack in a roasting pan. Roast until the chicken is done and the juices run clear (vertical roasting of a whole bird will take about 1 hour; roasting a whole bird on its back on a rack will take 1 hour 15 minutes; chicken parts will take 35 to 45 minutes). Let chicken stand 10 minutes before carving.

MEDITERRANEAN ROAST CHICKEN

Inspired by a James Beard and Craig Claiborne recipe for turkey, this combination of flavors seasons the chicken so wonderfully, it is as good cold as it is hot from the oven. Prepare the master recipe, using the following as the glaze: Combine 1 1/2 tablespoons herb blend, 1 tablespoon paprika, 1 tablespoon garlic paste, and 4 tablespoons olive oil in a small bowl. Rub paste all over the chicken and under the skin of the breast and leg (be careful not to tear the skin). Proceed with the master recipe.

TERIYAKI ROAST CHICKEN

Prepare the master recipe, brushing the chicken with 1/2 cup teriyaki glaze.

CARIBBEAN ROAST CHICKEN

Prepare the master recipe using the following as the glaze: Combine 2 tablespoons achiote paste with 1/3 cup water or wine in a blender or food processor.

INDONESIAN ROAST CHICKEN

Prepare the master recipe, coating the chicken with 1/2 cup peanut sauce (more or less, depending on the consistency of the sauce; thin with water or stock if necessary).

MUSTARD ROAST CHICKEN

Adapted from a Julia Child recipe, this combination invites you to use the wildest and spiciest mustard as the glaze because cooking mellows its pungency. Prepare the master recipe, using mustard to coat the chicken. A cup or so of mustard will coat a whole chicken. You can remove the chicken's skin if you like and apply the mustard to the flesh. If roasting chicken parts, you will need at least 1 1/2 cups mustard.

TURKEY *or* CHICKEN BREAST ESCALLOPS SAUTÉ

serves 4

Also known as paillards, escallops are thin, boneless slices that are very easy to prepare. When my family and I were camping in France for six weeks, we ate this sauté several times a week. Each time it was different, depending on the wine or sauce we had on hand for making a pan sauce. Dredging the escallops in flour helps thicken thin liquids like wine and stock, but isn't necessary for tomato or curry sauces. Skinned and boned chicken breasts or thighs may be substituted for the escallops, but they will take 6 to 8 minutes longer to cook.

2 tablespoons all-purpose flour (optional)

1 pound chicken or turkey breast, sliced into thin escallops

2 tablespoons canola, safflower, olive, or a flavored oil

Salt and ground black or white pepper

3/4 to 1 cup stock, wine, or sauce

If using the flour, place it on a plate and dredge the escallops in it before putting them in the pan. In a skillet over high heat, warm the oil. Quickly brown the escallops on both sides. Pour off any fat. Season escallops with salt and pepper and pour in the liquid. Bring to a boil and cook until the sauce is the desired consistency, but not longer than 3 to 4 minutes, so the meat isn't overcooked. Scrape up any crusty bits of food from the pan bottom and mix with sauce. If the sauce is too thin, remove the escallops, and boil the sauce until reduced and thickened. Return escallops to the pan and heat to serving temperature.

ITALIAN ESCALLOPS SAUTÉ

Prepare the master recipe, using the flour and 1 cup white wine. Add 1 teaspoon Italian herb blend with the liquid.

ESCALLOPS SAUTÉ WITH CURRY SAUCE

Prepare the master recipe but omit the flour. For the liquid, use 1 1/2 cups Indian or Thai curry sauce, or 2 tablespoons curry paste with 1 cup coconut milk or stock, or dredge the escallops in 1 to 2 tablespoons curry powder and use 1 cup of stock.

INDONESIAN ESCALLOPS SAUTÉ

Prepare the master recipe, but omit the flour. Use 1 cup coconut milk for the liquid and add 2 to 3 tablespoons fresh lime juice, 3 tablespoons peanut sauce, and 1 teaspoon sweet chili sauce.

ASIAN ESCALLOPS SAUTÉ

Prepare the master recipe, but omit the flour. Use 1/2 cup teriyaki or Szechuan sauce for the liquid and cook until the escallops are glazed with the sauce.

ESCALLOPS SAUTÉ COOK'S CHOICE

Prepare the master recipe but omit the flour. Use 1 cup white wine for the liquid and add one of the following: 1 tablespoon Dijon-style or flavored mustard, 2 tablespoons pesto, 2 tablespoons red pepper spread, 2 tablespoons tomato paste plus 1 teaspoon herb blend, or 2 tablespoons artichoke paste plus 1/2 teaspoon garlic paste. Finish as directed.

CHICKEN STEW

serves 4 to 6

CHICKEN STEW I

This boiled chicken stew is terrific on a cold, rainy day. Top it with refrigerator biscuit dough, cover, and bake on the stove top or in the oven, and you have chicken and dumplings. Leftovers are perfect for enchiladas, fajitas, sandwiches, rice dishes, and salads.

1 chicken, 4 pounds

2 celery stalks, sliced

2 carrots, sliced

1 onion, chopped

2 garlic cloves, minced, or **1 teaspoon garlic paste**

1 bay leaf

1 tablespoon herb blend

2 teaspoons salt

1/2 teaspoon ground white or black pepper

Fresh parsley, chopped

In a large soup pot, combine all of the ingredients except the parsley. Add water to cover and bring to a boil. Reduce the heat to low and simmer, covered, until the chicken is tender, 45 to 60 minutes. Remove the bay leaf. Carve the chicken into serving pieces or remove the meat from the bones (save bones for stock, page 69) and return to the pot to serve. Garnish with chopped parsley.

CHICKEN STEW II

This sautéed version assumes extra depth of flavor because the chicken is first browned in a little oil until golden. It requires less simmering as the pieces are already partially cooked from browning.

2 tablespoons canola, safflower, or olive oil

1 chicken, 4 pounds, cut into serving pieces and skinned

2 celery stalks, sliced

2 carrots, sliced

1 onion, chopped

2 garlic cloves, minced, or 1 teaspoon garlic paste

2 tablespoons all-purpose flour

2 to 4 cups stock, canned broth, sauce, or wine

1 bay leaf

1 tablespoon herb blend

Salt and ground black or white pepper

Fresh parsley or other fresh herb, for garnish

In a large Dutch oven or deep skillet over high heat, warm the oil. Brown the chicken, a few pieces at a time, and remove to a plate. Pour off all but 2 tablespoons fat. Sauté the celery, carrots, and onion until softened, 3 to 4 minutes. Stir in the garlic and flour and sauté 30 seconds. Return the chicken to the pan. Add the liquid, bay leaf, herb blend, and salt and pepper to taste. Bring to a boil, reduce the heat to medium-low, and simmer, covered, until the chicken is tender, 35 to 45 minutes. Garnish with chopped parsley.

CHICKEN CACCIATORE

Follow Chicken Stew II, with these changes: Sauté 1 cup sliced mushrooms with the other vegetables. For the liquid, use 2 cups mushroom pasta sauce and 1/2 cup white wine, plus an Italian herb blend. Optionally, add 1/4 cup olive salad. Garnish with chopped fresh basil and serve over pasta.

BELGIAN CHICKEN STEW WITH DRIED FRUIT

Follow Chicken Stew II, with these changes: Substitute rabbit for the chicken, if desired. For the liquid, use 2 cups rich chicken stock or 2 tablespoons glace de poulet and 2 cups water, plus 2 tablespoons red wine vinegar. Soak 1 cup (about 12) pitted prunes and 3/4 cup raisins in 1/3 cup cognac or brandy while the chicken is cooking. For the herb blend use fines herbes or other favorite blend that includes thyme. After the chicken has cooked for 30 minutes, stir in the prunes, raisins, and cognac. Raise the heat to high and boil rapidly to reduce and thicken the sauce. If the chicken is done before the sauce has thickened, remove the chicken and keep warm, and continue to boil down the sauce. Serve with rice or pasta.

MEXICAN CHICKEN STEW

Follow either Chicken Stew I or II, with these changes: Omit the herb blend. For the liquid, use 3 to 6 tablespoons mole paste (to taste) and 3 cups chicken stock. Garnish with toasted sesame seeds. Serve with rice.

MOROCCAN CHICKEN STEW

Follow Chicken Stew II, using chicken stock for the liquid. With the flour and garlic stir in 1 tablespoon Middle Eastern spice blend or za'atar. To the pot add 1 to 2 tablespoons hot or mild ajvar and 1 teaspoon grated lemon zest or 1 to 2 dried tangerine peels, minced. Garnish with chopped fresh parsley and serve over couscous.

WEST AFRICAN CHICKEN STEW

Follow Chicken Stew II, with these changes: When the flour is added, also add 1 1/2 teaspoons cayenne pepper or other ground chile. For the herbs, add 2 teaspoons dried oregano leaves and 1 teaspoon ground ginger. For the liquid, use 2 cups (or one 16-ounce can) chopped tomatoes with their juice and 1 cup chicken stock, broth, or water. Stir in 3 to 4 tablespoons creamy peanut butter or 1/4 cup African peanut sauce. Serve over rice.

MADRAS CHICKEN STEW

Follow either Chicken Stew I or II, with these changes: Omit the herb blend. Use 3 tablespoons curry blend with tamarind or combine 2 to 3 tablespoons tamarind paste with 3 tablespoons curry paste. For the liquid, use 2 cups stock, broth, or plain yogurt. Garnish with chopped fresh parsley.

CHICKEN STEW VINDALOO

Follow either Chicken Stew I or II, with these changes: Omit the herb blend. For the sauce, combine vindaloo paste or seasoning blend according to the package directions, using stock, broth, or water for the liquid. Add 2 cups cubed potatoes to the mixture and cook as directed.

SEASONED
MEAT LOAF *or* PATTIES

serves 4 to 6

Herb blends, mustard, and a variety of pastes perk up everyday ground loaves and patties. Here are some suggestions and proportions to spur you on to your own creations. Leftover meat loaf or patties, cut up into chunks, become meatballs for pasta sauces or sandwich makings.

2 pounds ground beef, pork, or lamb, in any combination

1 onion, chopped

2 garlic cloves, or 1 teaspoon garlic paste

1 egg

1/2 cup dried bread crumbs or uncooked oatmeal

Salt and freshly ground black pepper

1/2 cup ketchup or other sauce (optional)

Preheat the oven to 375 degrees F. In a mixing bowl, combine the ground meat with all the ingredients except ketchup (if using). Mix well and form into a loaf or divide evenly into 8 to 10 patties. Set in a baking pan. Spread ketchup or other sauce (if using) over the top of the meat and bake until the juices run clear, 45 to 60 minutes for a loaf, 30 to 40 minutes for patties. Serve with more sauce, if you like.

JAMAICAN MEAT LOAF OR PATTIES

Prepare the master recipe using half ground beef and half ground pork. Stir in 2 to 3 tablespoons jerk seasoning. Instead of a loaf or patties, the mixture can be made into meatballs, browned in a skillet, and finished in 1 1/2 cups coconut milk.

MIDDLE EASTERN MEAT LOAF OR PATTIES

Prepare the master recipe using ground lamb or ground beef with these changes: Substitute 3/4 cup falafel mix for the bread crumbs. Mix in 1/2 cup plain yogurt or milk to keep the meat moist. For the ketchup, substitute 3 to 4 tablespoons hot or mild ajvar or 1/2 cup plain yogurt.

CREOLE MEAT LOAF OR PATTIES

Prepare the master recipe with these changes: Add 1/2 green bell pepper, seeded and chopped; 1 to 2 teaspoons Creole or Cajun herb blend; and Tabasco or other Louisiana hot sauce to taste. Omit the ketchup and serve with a Creole sauce.

TERIYAKI MEAT LOAF OR PATTIES

Prepare the master recipe with these changes: Add 2/3 cup teriyaki sauce to the meat mixture. Omit the ketchup, but brush more teriyaki sauce over the meat, basting occasionally during cooking to develop a glaze.

SWEET-AND-SOUR MEAT LOAF OR PATTIES

Prepare the master recipe, but substitute 3/4 cup sweet-and-sour sauce for the ketchup.

SUN-DRIED TOMATO MEAT LOAF OR PATTIES

Prepare the master recipe and stir in 1/2 cup sun-dried tomato relish or 1/4 cup finely chopped sun-dried tomatoes.

MEAT STEW

serves 4

Beef, lamb, and pork are meaty canvases upon which to star the boldest ingredients from any cuisine. In cultures where small amounts of meat are eaten, highly seasoned stews, goulashes, garbures, and curries are filled with vegetables and potatoes, or top big helpings of rice or pasta.

3 tablespoons all-purpose flour

Salt and freshly ground black pepper

2 teaspoons herb or spice blend (or a blend of $1/2$ teaspoon salt, $1/4$ teaspoon freshly ground black pepper, and $1/4$ teaspoon paprika)

2 pounds beef, lamb, or pork, cut into 1-inch cubes

3 tablespoons canola or safflower oil

1 onion, chopped

1 to 2 carrots, chopped

2 garlic cloves, chopped, or 1 teaspoon garlic paste

3 cups stock, canned broth, or wine, in any combination; or a sauce

1 bay leaf

In a bowl or paper bag, combine the flour with salt and pepper to taste and herbs or spices. Dredge the meat in the mixture and set aside on a plate. In a heavy Dutch oven or deep skillet over high heat, warm the oil. Brown the meat, a few pieces at a time. Remove to a plate as they brown and continue until all the meat is browned. Add the onion and carrots to the pan and sauté until softened, about 3 minutes. Add the garlic and sauté another 30 seconds.

(continued at right)

Return the meat to the pan and stir in the stock or wine and the bay leaf. Bring to a boil, reduce the heat to medium, cover, and simmer until the meat is tender and the sauce is thickened, about 1¹/₂ hours, stirring occasionally. Remove bay leaf. Serve over mashed potatoes, rice, or pasta.

HUNGARIAN BEEF GOULASH

Prepare the master recipe using beef with these changes: For the seasoning use 2 teaspoons paprika and 1 teaspoon goulash herb blend or other favorite blend. For the liquid use 1 cup dry white wine, 2 cups (or one 16-ounce can) chopped tomatoes with their juices, and 2 tablespoons tomato paste. After the meat simmers 45 minutes, stir in another teaspoon paprika; 3 potatoes, peeled and quartered; and 1¹/₂ cups sauerkraut (rinsed, if canned). Cook until all ingredients are tender, another 30 to 45 minutes. Garnish with snipped fresh chives and sour cream, if you like.

MOROCCAN LAMB TAJINE

Prepare the master recipe using lamb with these changes: For the seasoning add 1 tablespoon Moroccan herb and spice blend or za'atar. For the liquid use 2 cups (or one 16-ounce can) chopped tomatoes with their juices, 3 tablespoons tomato paste, and ³/₄ to 1 cup stock, broth, or water. Sauté 2 Japanese eggplants, unpeeled and chopped, with the onion and carrots. Garnish with toasted almonds and serve over couscous.

BRAZILIAN COZIDO

Prepare the master recipe using beef and/or pork with these changes: For the seasoning, use a Latin American herb or spice blend or add 1 teaspoon coriander and ¹/₂ teaspoon ground dried green chile (such as *habanero*) powder. For the liquid, use beef stock, canned beef broth, or water. After the stew has cooked for 45 minutes, add to the stew 1 pound sweet potato or yams, peeled and cut into cubes; 4 tomatoes, chopped; ¹/₄ head green cabbage, shredded; and ¹/₄ pound linguica, sliced and sautéed. Optionally, stir in ¹/₄ pound whole or sliced fresh or thawed frozen okra. Garnish with chopped fresh cilantro and lime wedges. Serve with tomato salsa.

CHILE BEEF WITH ARTICHOKE HEARTS

This recipe is adapted from a book on casseroles published by *Sunset* magazine. Prepare the master recipe using beef with these changes: For the liquid, use half red wine and half stock. Use a Mexican herb or spice blend. With the liquid, stir in one 3 1/2-ounce can (1/3 cup) chopped green chiles. After the stew has cooked for 45 minutes, stir in 1 cup marinated artichoke hearts, drained. Optionally, add 1 cup pearl onions. Garnish with chopped fresh cilantro and serve over rice or pasta.

EAST AFRICAN STEW

Prepare the master recipe using beef or lamb with these changes: Blend 1/2 teaspoon or more berberé seasoning with the flour. Use beef stock or water for the liquid, plus 2 cups (or one 16-ounce can) chopped tomatoes with their juice. Also add 2 cups more chopped vegetables such as celery, cauliflower, yams, cassava, and peas. Optionally, stir in 1 cup cooked garbanzo beans or millet. Garnish with chopped fresh cilantro or parsley.

PORK ADOBO

Prepare the master recipe using pork with these changes: For the seasoning, blend chili powder or other Mexican seasoning with the flour. For the liquid, use 2 cups stock, broth, or water; 1 cup chopped fresh or canned tomatoes; and 1 cup adobo sauce. Garnish with chopped fresh cilantro. Serve in warm corn tortillas with sour cream or plain yogurt.

WEST AFRICAN PEANUT STEW

Prepare the master recipe using lamb or beef with these changes: With the flour, add 1 1/2 teaspoons cayenne pepper or other ground dried chile. For the herbs, add 2 teaspoons dried oregano leaves and 1 teaspoon ground ginger. For the liquid, use 2 cups (or one 16-ounce can) chopped tomatoes, with their juice, and 1 cup beef stock, canned beef broth, or water. After the stew has cooked for 45 minutes, stir in 3 to 4 tablespoons creamy peanut butter or 1/4 cup African peanut sauce. Serve over rice.

Prepare the master recipe using lamb with these changes: From 2 to 12 hours ahead, rub the meat with $1/2$ cup biryani paste and marinate. Omit the flour dredging and proceed with browning the onion and carrots. Add the meat and marinade, plus 1 cup stock, broth, or water; cook as directed until tender, about 1 hour. Serve over rice, or layer in a baked rice dish.

PANTRY
EQUIVALENTS

MEAT AND POULTRY

A 4-pound chicken equals 4 to 5 servings

$1/4$ to $1/3$ cup paste or herb blend will cover a 4-pound chicken
(double it if the chicken is cut up)

$1/4$ cup paste or rub will cover 3 pounds of meat for the grill

$1^1/2$ pounds pork ribs equals 1 entrée serving

4 to 6 ounces of boneless meat per entrée serving if grilled or roasted;
3 to 5 ounces for stews and fajitas

2 to 3 chicken parts equals 1 entrée serving

CURRY

serves 4

Here is an example of a commercial sauce becoming the ultimate convenience food. Take a look at the number of ingredients on a jar of Indian, Thai, or Caribbean curry sauce and be glad someone else has gone to the trouble of combining them. If, instead of a jar of sauce, you prefer to keep curry powder or paste on the shelf, directions for using them are given in the variations. As always, taste a sauce or seasoning before you use it to determine how much to add.

2 tablespoons canola or safflower oil

3 pounds favorite chicken parts, skinned; 1 1/2 pounds boned chicken thighs or breast; or lamb or beef, cubed

1 onion, sliced

1 bell pepper (or 1/2 red and 1/2 green bell pepper), seeded and sliced

1 3/4 cups (or one 14-ounce can) **curry sauce**

1/2 to 1 cup water, depending on sauce

Optional accompaniments: chutney, sliced bananas, chopped tomatoes, chopped roasted peanuts, grated unsweetened coconut, lime wedges

(continued at right)

In a deep skillet over high heat, warm the oil. Brown the chicken or meat cubes, a few pieces at a time, and remove from the skillet. When all the meat is browned, sauté the onion and bell pepper until softened. Remove vegetables and pour off the fat from the skillet. Stir in the curry sauce and water. Bring to a boil. Return the chicken or meat and vegetables to the pan and finish cooking, 20 to 30 minutes.

Alternatively, place the browned chicken or meat and vegetables in a baking dish. Preheat the oven to 350 degrees F. Bring the curry sauce and water to a boil in the pan and pour it over the contents of the baking dish. Cover with aluminum foil and bake in the oven until tender, 30 minutes (for chicken) to 1 hour or so (for meat).

WITH CURRY POWDER Brown the chicken or meat as directed in the master recipe and remove from the pan. When the onion and pepper are softened, add 1 to 3 tablespoons curry powder (to taste) and sauté 1 minute longer. Stir in 1 1/2 cups stock, canned broth, coconut milk, or water and bring to a boil. Return the chicken to the pan and either finish on top of the stove or in the oven as directed in the master recipe.

WITH CURRY PASTE Brown the chicken or meat as directed in the master recipe and remove from the pan. For the liquid, stir in 1/4 to 1/2 cup curry paste (to taste) and 1 1/4 cups stock, canned broth, coconut milk, or water. Continue as directed in the master recipe.

THAI CURRY

Follow the master recipe with these changes: For the curry sauce use 1 to 3 tablespoons (to taste) red, green, or yellow curry seasoning and 1 3/4 cups (or one 14-ounce can) coconut milk. Stir in 1 tablespoon fish sauce and proceed as directed. Garnish with chopped tomatoes, lime wedges, chopped roasted peanuts, and fried basil leaves.

VINDALOO

At least 4 hours or overnight, marinate lamb or chicken in a vindaloo spice mixture, or in a combination of 2 tablespoons of curry powder, 1/2 cup distilled white or cider vinegar, and 3 tablespoons canola oil. Proceed as directed in the master recipe and, since the meat is already highly seasoned, add the curry sauce to taste. This is a hot curry, so go heavy on the spices. Serve over rice.

CARIBBEAN CURRY

For a treat like you might have in Jamaica, substitute goat for the the chicken. Follow the directions for curry powder and use coconut milk for the liquid. Garnish with chopped avocado, lime wedges, and chopped mango, papaya, and bananas.

PANTRY
TIPS

Add leftover cooked chicken or meat to rice and pasta dishes such as Skillet and Stir-Fried Rice, page 152, Baked Rice, page 156, or Thai Peanut Noodles, page 148.

Cut leftover meat loaf into cubes to use as meatballs for pasta sauces. When the meat cooks in the sauce for about 15 minutes, the square corners round off and the meat lends its flavor to the sauce.

FAJITAS

serves 6 to 8

Weekly fare at my house, fajitas can be made with either fresh or leftover cooked chicken, pork, or beef. Two seasoning blends are used in this recipe, but fajita seasoning can be substituted in both places.

2 pounds boneless pork shoulder, beef sirloin, or chicken thighs

2 tablespoons Southwestern spice rub or 1/4 cup marinade

2 tablespoons canola or safflower oil

1/2 red bell pepper, seeded and sliced

1/2 green bell pepper, seeded and sliced

1/2 onion, sliced

1 garlic clove, minced, or 1/4 teaspoon garlic paste

2 to 3 tablespoons fajita seasoning

1/4 cup water

12 to 16 corn tortillas

Oil for frying

Chopped tomatoes, salsa, and/or guacamole, for garnish

To prepare the meat: Preheat the oven to 450 degrees F. Pat the meat all over with the spice rub or brush with marinade. Place in a cast-iron skillet (use one with ribs on the inside bottom to mark the meat with grill marks) or a roasting pan, and set it in the oven. Reduce heat to 375 degrees F. Roast until cooked through: chicken, 20 minutes; beef, 25 to 30 minutes; pork, 30 to 40 minutes. Remove from the oven and let stand 5 minutes. Slice meat into thin strips about 1/2 inch wide.

(continued at right)

To make the fajita filling: In a skillet over medium-high heat, warm the oil. Sauté bell peppers and onion until soft. Add the garlic and fajita seasoning and sauté for 1 minute. Stir in the water and cook 5 minutes longer to blend the seasonings. Stir in the meat and reheat.

For the tortillas, heat oil to a depth of $1/4$ inch in a small skillet. Fry tortillas quickly to keep them soft, turning once with tongs. Remove and drain on paper towels. Alternatively, heat flour tortillas wrapped in plastic in the microwave on high for 2 minutes or wrapped in foil in the oven at 350 degrees F for 10 to 12 minutes. Keep warm. To serve, spoon fajita mixture into the tortillas and top with tomatoes, salsa, and guacamole, as desired.

FAJITAS WITH ACHIOTE PASTE

When preparing the meat for cooking, use 2 to 3 tablespoons achiote paste diluted in $1/4$ cup water for the spice rub.

MEAT MARINADE FAJITAS

When preparing the meat for cooking, use $1/4$ cup meat marinade for the Southwestern spice rub.

CHICKEN *and* MEAT ON THE GRILL

serves 4 to 6

The smoky flavor of grilled food pairs with some of the most outrageous sauces on the market, from jerk to barbecue. Some of my favorite dinners have been those with an international barbecue theme. Note that the meat must marinate up to a day ahead before grilling.

2 to 3 pounds pork shoulder; 3 to 4 pounds chicken parts; 2 to 3 pounds beef tenderloin, sirloin, or London Broil; 2 to 3 pounds lamb leg or shoulder; or 2 to 3 pounds of beef, lamb, or pork steaks, chops, or fillets; or beef cut into 2-inch cubes for skewering

1/2 cup dry seasoning rub or 1 cup barbecue sauce

The night before cooking, or at least 4 hours ahead, rub the meat or chicken with the seasoning or sauce and refrigerate. About an hour before cooking, remove meat or chicken from the refrigerator. Prepare a barbecue. When the coals are hot, grill the meat until cooked to desired doneness. Pork will take 45 to 60 minutes; chicken, 35 to 45 minutes; beef tenderloin, sirloin of London Broil, 25 to 40 minutes; steaks, chops, or fillets, 20 to 30 minutes; skewers, 20 to 30 minute; lamb, 35 to 45 minutes. Turn the meat once or twice while cooking. To get the most smoky flavor, cover the grill, and once the meat is browned, move pieces next to, not over, the hot coals, for the remainder of cooking. If using barbecue sauce, pass extra sauce with the cooked meat.

CARIBBEAN JERK GRILL

Some jerk sauces are exceptionally hot and may be diluted with a little water to make a marinade rather than a rub. Use ⅓ cup jerk seasoning paste for the rub and marinate the meat or chicken parts overnight. Grill as directed in the master recipe.

GRILLED JERKED DRUMETTES

Marinate 2 to 3 pounds chicken drumettes (the two parts of the wing that are meaty) overnight. Grill as directed in the master recipe for about 20 minutes.

LATIN AMERICAN ACHIOTE GRILL

Similar to Peruvian *anticucho*, these are skewers of beef. Slice 1½ pounds beef sirloin across the grain into paper-thin strips (freezing the meat for a few hours eases this process), then lay strips in a shallow baking dish. In a food processor or blender, combine and puree 1 cup red wine, ¼ cup water, 2 tablespoons oil, 1½ teaspoons garlic paste, 3 tablespoons achiote paste, 1 teaspoon crushed red pepper, salt and freshly ground black pepper (to taste), and 1 pasilla chile, soaked in boiling water for 20 minutes (optional). Pour over the meat, cover, and refrigerate 6 to 8 hours or overnight.

Thread meat, 3 to 4 pieces at a time, on each of twenty-four 8-inch bamboo skewers soaked in water 15 to 20 minutes. Grill as directed in the master recipe for about 5 minutes, basting with the marinade.

SENEGALESE YASSA

Use 1½ pounds lean beef or chicken, cut into 1-inch cubes. For the marinade combine ½ cup fresh lemon or lime juice, 2 tablespoons canola or safflower oil (or a lemon- or garlic-infused oil), 1 teaspoon chile paste, 1 teaspoon garlic paste, and salt and freshly ground black pepper to taste. Marinate at least 1 hour (up to overnight for the beef, up to 4 hours for the chicken). Thread the meat alternately with 1-inch squares of onion on 16 to 20 bamboo skewers soaked in water 15 to 20 minutes. Grill over hot coals as directed in the master recipe until cooked through, 6 to 10 minutes. Pour any remaining marinade in a saucepan and boil 2 to 3 minutes to serve with the meat. Serve with tomato salsa.

GRILLED SOUTHEAST ASIAN PORK STICKS

Ground meat is typically skewered, grilled, and served wrapped in lettuce leaves in Vietnam, Cambodia, and parts of Thailand. Use 2 pounds lean ground pork and season it with a Southeast Asian spice mixture or a mixture of 2 tablespoons soy sauce; 1 tablespoon oil; 1 tablespoon hot chili oil; 1 tablespoon fresh lemon or lime juice; 1 teaspoon garlic paste; 2 teaspoons minced peeled ginger; 3/4 teaspoon sugar; and 2 green onions, including green tops, chopped. Mix well and form into twelve 3-inch cylinders. Insert a bamboo skewer soaked in water 15 to 20 minutes into each. Grill over hot coals as directed in the master recipe until cooked through, 15 to 20 minutes. Serve wrapped in lettuce leaves with Thai or other Asian dipping sauce.

SOUTHWESTERN GRILL

Prepare the master recipe using 3 pounds pork shoulder or beef top sirloin. Season with 1/3 to 1/2 cup dry seasoning rub and refrigerate for at least 1 hour or up to overnight. Grill over hot coals as directed, 45 minutes for pork, 25 to 35 minutes for beef. Slice thinly and serve with salsa, chopped avocados, and chopped cilantro in warmed corn tortillas. Alternatively, serve the sliced meat with a favorite Southwestern barbecue sauce.

YAKITORI

Japan's fabulous grilled skewered chicken is typically made this way: From 1 to 12 hours in advance, marinate 1 1/2 pounds boned chicken thighs or breasts, cut into 1-inch cubes, in 1/2 cup teriyaki or other Asian glaze made with soy sauce. Thread 5 or 6 pieces of the meat on each of 16 to 18 bamboo skewers soaked in water for 15 to 20 minutes. Grill over hot coals as directed in the master recipe until cooked through, 10 to 15 minutes, basting with the marinade several times to give it the classic sticky yakitori glaze.

SATAY

To make the popular skewered chicken with peanut sauce from Indonesia, coat 1 1/2 pounds of boned chicken thighs or breasts, cut into 1-inch cubes, in 3/4 to 1 cup peanut sauce. If you have a thin peanut sauce, marinate the chicken in sauce for up to 4 hours. If it is thick, marinate 1 to 2 hours. Thread 5 or 6 pieces of the chicken on each of 16 to 18 bamboo skewers soaked in water 15 to 20 minutes. Grill over hot coals as directed in the master recipe until cooked through, 10 to 15 minutes, turning frequently to keep from burning. Serve with extra peanut sauce.

ALL-AMERICAN GRILL

Parboil 4 pounds pork ribs for 10 minutes. Drain them, pat dry, and rub them with 1/2 cup barbecue seasoning rub; or marinate in 1/2 to 3/4 cup barbecue sauce, and refrigerate 2 to 12 hours. Grill over hot coals as directed in the master recipe, turning once after 5 minutes. When both sides are browned, move the ribs next to, not over, the coals and baste, if you like. Cover the grill and cook to melt-in-your-mouth tenderness, 35 to 45 minutes.

GRILLED SZECHUAN RIBS

Place 3 pounds pork ribs, separated into individual ribs, 1 1/2 teaspoons garlic paste, and 1 tablespoon chopped peeled ginger in a saucepan with water to cover. Boil until ribs are tender, 30 to 40 minutes. Drain. Lay the hot ribs on a baking sheet and brush with Szechuan sauce on both sides. (If time permits, refrigerate them at this point up to overnight.) Grill as directed in the All-American Grill (preceding). Or, preheat the oven to 425 degrees F, and roast ribs until glazed and browned, 25 to 30 minutes. When cooked, brush with the sauce again and serve. Serves 4.

GRILLED TURKEY DRUMS

Marinate 4 to 6 turkey drumsticks, skinned, in $1/2$ to $1/3$ cup teriyaki sauce, barbecue marinade, or jerk or other seasoning (or 1 in each!). Grill as directed in the master recipe until cooked through, turning occasionally, 35 to 45 minutes. Brush with the marinade several times. Or, preheat the oven to 400 degrees F and roast the turkey until cooked through, 35 to 45 minutes.

CHIMICHURRI GRILL

Rub chimichurri paste over beef steaks or pork chops, cover, and refrigerate up to overnight before grilling. Grill as directed in the master recipe.

TANDOORI GRILL

Marinate 3 pounds boneless chicken breasts in a mixture of $1/2$ cup plain yogurt, plus $1/4$ cup fresh lime or lemon juice, and 1 to 2 table-spoons tandoori herb and spice blend (with extra paprika if you like) or garam masala (without turmeric). Marinate 4 hours to overnight. Grill over hot coals as directed in the master recipe.

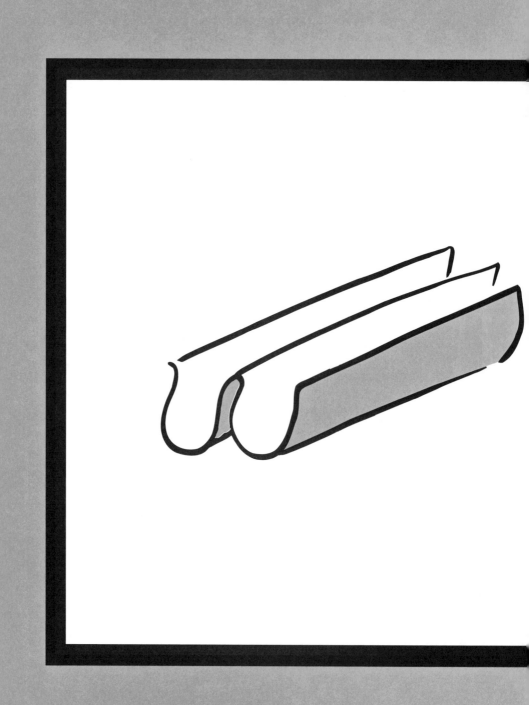

pizza, **bread**

biscuits + crêpes

Now we come to the ultimate conveniences. Reaching into the pantry for pasta sauce, olives, sun-dried tomatoes, roasted red pepper strips, artichoke hearts, pine nuts, and pesto has no greater reward than when these are served hot from the oven on a crusty **BREAD** or **PIZZA**. As with all of the recipes in this book, the pantry's the limit. I doubt that I've ever topped a pizza or crostini the same way twice, except when I was creating the ones in this chapter. Included are suggestions, but consider them guidelines. Always keep a premade pizza round or frozen pizza dough on hand. Think of yesterday's French bread for company appetizers or open-face sandwiches. I also share two more of my favorite bread bases - **BISCUITS**, flavored with herbs, olives, or sun-dried tomatoes, to serve with soup or stew, and seasoned **CRÊPES**, to fill with a meat or vegetable sauté. Enjoy.

Pizza Basics
page 226

Crostini
page 228

Garlic Bread
page 232

RECIPE
LIST

Biscuits
page 234

Crêpes
page 236

PIZZA BASICS

serves 2 to 4

This is once- or twice-a-week fare in my house, and often suffices for lunches on the run as well. Included are suggestions for fresh and pantry toppings. The choice is up to you. Using a pizza stone ensures a crisp crust.

16- to 18-inch partially baked pizza round; or frozen pizza dough, prebaked according to the package directions

2 to 3 tablespoons garlic- or herb-infused olive oil

1 to 1 1/2 cups pasta sauce

4 to 6 ounces grated or crumbled cheese such as mozzarella, goat cheese, fontina, and/or feta

Optional fresh toppings: sliced tomatoes, sliced red or green bell peppers, sliced cooked potatoes, sautéed zucchini, sautéed mushrooms, olives, arugula, spinach, sliced sausages, salami, ham, smoked chicken

Optional pantry toppings: olive salad, roasted red bell peppers, artichoke hearts or artichoke paste, caponata, aioli, sun-dried tomatoes, caramelized onions, pine nuts, fresh or dried herbs

Place pizza stone in oven, if using. Preheat the oven to 425 to 450 degrees F. Brush pizza dough with oil and place on a baking sheet. Spread sauce over the top. Sprinkle with cheese and top with choice of fresh and/or pantry toppings and herbs. Bake (slide pizza off the baking sheet and onto pizza stone if using) until cheese is melted and crust is browned, 15 to 20 minutes. Let stand a minute or two before cutting.

INTERNATIONAL HERB PIZZA

Give your pizza a Mexican, Asian, or Caribbean accent with 1 or 2 tablespoons of those herb blends sprinkled over it.

SEAFOOD PIZZA

Prepare the master recipe up to spooning on the pasta sauce. After the sauce is spooned on, top it with 1/4 pound scallops and 1/4 pound medium shrimp, shelled and deveined, sautéed in garlic-infused olive oil just until done. Add sliced red bell peppers, and dollops of pesto, goat cheese, and red pepper spread, then bake as directed.

PROVENÇAL PISSALADIÈRE

Before preparing the master recipe, in a skillet over medium-low heat, warm 2 tablespoons olive oil. Sauté 3 onions, thinly sliced, with 2 tablespoon herbes de Provence until very tender, 30 to 40 minutes. Prepare the master recipe up to spooning on the sauce. Brush pizza round with plain or flavored olive oil. Top with the onions. Dot with anchovy paste. Arrange 6 tomatoes, sliced, and 8 to 10 Niçoise olives over onions. Bake as directed.

PANTRY
TIP

Drop dots of anchovy paste, pesto, red pepper spread, artichoke paste, tapenade, or aioli onto pizza as a garnish just before baking.

CROSTINI

makes 12 crostini

Sliced day-old baguettes make expeditious appetizers. Most of these topping suggestions also improve crackers, English muffins, and bagels.

12 slices baguette, cut $1/2$ inch thick

$1/4$ cup olive oil, plain or flavored with garlic or herbs

Preheat oven to 400 degrees F. Brush baguette slices on both sides with olive oil and place on baking sheet. Bake 5 minutes. Remove and turn over if desired. If you choose not to turn over, the crusty side can either be the bottom or the top. Top with favorite ingredients or one of the following variations.

MEDITERRANEAN CROSTINI

Prepare the bread according to the master recipe. Spread each slice with a tablespoon or so of pasta primavera sauce, Italian-style salsa, or caponata. Top with a slice of tomato and sprinkle with grated Parmesan cheese and Italian herb blend. Bake an additional 5 minutes and serve hot.

OLIVE-MUSHROOM CROSTINI

Prepare the bread according to the master recipe. Spread each slice with a tablespoon or so of pasta sauce. Top with slices of mushrooms, a drop of tapenade, and a sprinkling of fines herbes. Bake an additional 5 minutes and serve hot.

CHEESE, BELL PEPPER, AND ARTICHOKE HEART CROSTINI

Prepare the bread according to the master recipe. Sprinkle each slice with grated Monterey jack or fontina cheese, or spread with 3 ounces of goat cheese. Top with slices of red bell pepper, a dollop of artichoke pesto or paste, and a slice of marinated artichoke. Bake an additional 5 minutes, sprinkle with chopped fresh parsley, and serve hot.

TOMATO-MOZZARELLA CROSTINI

Prepare the bread according to the master recipe. Spread each slice with a tablespoon or so of sun-dried tomato relish or tomato basil pasta sauce. Top with grated mozzarella cheese, a slice of tomato, and a sprinkling of fresh or dried herbs or a dollop of pesto. Bake an additional 5 minutes and serve hot.

MUSTARD-MOZZARELLA CROSTINI

Prepare the bread according to the master recipe. Spread each slice with 1 to 2 teaspoons Dijon-style or other favorite mustard. Top with grated mozzarella cheese, several thin slices of tomatoes, and half a pitted kalamata olive.

GOAT CHEESE-BALSAMIC ONION CROSTINI

Prepare the bread according to the master recipe. Spread each slice with 1 to 2 tablespoons goat cheese, top with a tablespoon of balsamic onion relish and serve.

CREAM CHEESE-RED PEPPER CROSTINI

Prepare the bread according to the master recipe. Spread each slice with 1 to 2 tablespoons cream cheese and top with a tablespoon of red pepper spread. Garnish with chopped fresh basil and serve.

BAY SHRIMP CROSTINI

Prepare the bread according to the master recipe. Combine 1/2 cup softened cream cheese with 1/4 pound cooked bay shrimp and 2 tablespoons red pepper spread or 1 teaspoon dill mustard. Spread on each slice of toasted bread, top with a dab of pesto or chopped fresh parsley, and serve.

CURRIED CRAB CROSTINI

Prepare the bread according to the master recipe. Combine 1/2 cup mayonnaise with 1 to 2 teaspoons curry paste and 1/4 pound crab meat. Spread on each slice of toasted bread, top with a fresh cilantro leaf, and serve.

CRAB-TOMATO CROSTINI

Prepare the bread according to the master recipe. Combine 1/4 pound crab meat with 2 tablespoons tomato or other salad dressing and 1 to 2 ounces softened cream cheese. Spread on each slice of toasted bread, sprinkle with snipped fresh chives, and serve.

PANTRY
TIP

Use 1 to 2 teaspoons of concentrated
relishes such as tapenade, olive salad, or red pepper spread on
each cracker or crostini for appetizers. A 4- to
6-ounce jar will make about 24 servings, depending on the
concentration of the sauce.

GARLIC BREAD

serves 8 to 12

Comforting and filling, garlic bread is a way to use loaves of bread that are past their initial freshness. Use regular garlic paste for a strong garlic taste, and roasted garlic paste for a more mellow flavor. Alternatively, find a powdered garlic mix and stir it into olive oil or melted butter.

1/2 cup butter, or 1/4 cup butter and 1/4 cup safflower, canola, or garlic-infused oil

2 to 3 garlic cloves, minced or 1 to 1 1/2 teaspoons garlic paste

1 teaspoon fresh lemon juice (optional)

1 loaf French bread, halved lengthwise

Preheat the broiler. In a small saucepan over medium-low heat, melt the butter and add the garlic. Cook a minute or so, but don't brown butter. Stir in lemon juice (if using). Brush both bread halves with garlic butter, place them on a baking sheet, and broil until tops are bubbly and beginning to brown, 3 to 5 minutes. Serve hot.

HERBED GARLIC BREAD

Prepare the master recipe as directed, stirring 1 to 2 tablespoons fines herbes, Italian, or other favorite herb blend into the melted butter. Alternatively, sprinkle the herbs over the bread after it has browned and just before serving.

TAPENADE-TOPPED GARLIC BREAD

Prepare the master recipe as directed. Remove bread from the oven and spread with 1/2 cup tapenade. Sprinkle with chopped fresh parsley and serve.

SUN-DRIED TOMATO GARLIC BREAD

Prepare the master recipe as directed. Remove bread from the oven and spread with 1/2 cup sun-dried tomato pesto.

RED PEPPER-GOAT CHEESE GARLIC BREAD

Prepare the master recipe as directed. Remove bread from the oven and spread a thin layer of fresh goat cheese (2 to 3 ounces) over the bread. Dollop 1/3 cup of red pepper spread over the goat cheese and broil 2 to 3 minutes. Garnish with chopped fresh or dried basil.

OLIVE GARLIC BREAD

Prepare the master recipe as directed. Remove bread from the oven and spread with 1/2 cup olive salad or olive relish.

BISCUITS

makes about twelve 3-inch biscuits

Next to purchased bread, biscuits are the ultimate quick bread. Here is a basic recipe followed by pantry selections to make these light, tender rolls stand on their own with mellow soups and salads.

4 cups all-purpose flour

3 tablespoons baking powder

3/4 teaspoon salt

1/2 teaspoon sugar (optional)

1/3 cup solid vegetable shortening or butter

1 1/4 cups milk or buttermilk

1/4 cup butter (optional)

Preheat the oven to 400 degrees F. In a mixing bowl, combine the flour, baking powder, salt, and sugar (if using). Cut in the shortening using a pastry blender, 2 knives, or your fingers until the mixture is mealy. Pour in the milk and stir until the dough holds together in a rough mass. Turn out onto a lightly floured board and knead gently. Pat or roll out the dough 1/2 to 3/4 inch thick. Using a 3-inch biscuit cutter or glass, cut out rounds. Place the rounds on greased baking sheets. Pat the scraps together and cut out as many more biscuits as possible. The last biscuit is formed by hand. Bake until biscuits have risen and are lightly browned on top, 15 to 20 minutes. If you like, rub butter over the tops of the biscuits hot out of the oven.

HERB BISCUITS

Prepare the master recipe as directed, stirring 1 tablespoon dried oregano, basil, sage, parsley, or herb or curry blend into the dry ingredients.

CHILI-CORN BISCUITS

Prepare the master recipe with these changes: Substitute 1 cup fine cornmeal for 1 cup of the flour and stir 1 tablespoon chili powder into the dry ingredients.

SUN-DRIED TOMATO BISCUITS

Prepare the master recipe as directed, stirring 1/4 cup chopped sun-dried tomatoes or 1/3 cup sun-dried tomato pesto into the dry ingredients.

OLIVE BISCUITS

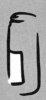

Prepare the master recipe as directed, stirring 1/4 cup chopped olives or 1/3 cup tapenade into the dry ingredients.

FILLED BISCUITS

Prepare the master recipe with these changes: Pat the dough 1/2 inch thick and cut out the biscuits. Place one round of dough on a greased baking sheet and spread with 1/2 teaspoon sun-dried tomato relish, tapenade, pesto, or other relish or paste. Top with a second biscuit. Repeat until all the dough is used. Brush the tops with butter before baking. Bake for 18 to 25 minutes. Makes about 8 filled biscuits.

CRÊPES

makes about fourteen 6-inch crêpes

These delights are terrific stuffed with a creamy cheese or vegetable relish, or eaten plain like bread.

3 eggs

$1/2$ teaspoon salt

$1/4$ cup vegetable oil

$1^1/4$ cups all-purpose flour

$1^1/2$ cups milk

2 tablespoons butter

Beat eggs in a mixing bowl or food processor. Mix in the salt, oil, flour, and milk and beat until smooth. Let stand 15 to 20 minutes. In a 6-inch skillet over medium-high heat, warm a dab of the butter until it melts and sizzles. Pour in enough crêpe batter to coat the bottom of the pan thinly. When the batter sets, turn the crêpe over with a spatula or your fingers and quickly brown the other side. Remove from the pan and continue cooking the rest of the crêpes in the same way until all of the batter is used. Serve warm. Alternatively, stuff the crêpes with a filling, lay them in a shallow dish, dot with additional dabs of butter, cover with foil, and bake in an oven preheated to 350 degrees F until heated through, 15 to 20 minutes.

HERB CRÊPES

Prepare the master recipe as directed, stirring 2 to 3 tablespoons herb blend and 1 tablespoon finely chopped fresh parsley into the batter. Proceed as directed. Serve hot.

CURRIED CRÊPES

Prepare the master recipe as directed, stirring 2 tablespoons curry powder into the batter. Proceed as directed. On each crêpe, spread 1 to 2 tablespoons softened cream cheese and 1 to 2 tablespoons chutney and roll up. Serve at room temperature.

RED PEPPER CRÊPES

Prepare the master recipe as directed, stirring 1/2 teaspoon cayenne pepper into the batter. Proceed as directed. On each crêpe, spread 1 to 2 tablespoons red pepper relish or sun-dried tomato pesto and roll up. Serve at room temperature.

MEXICAN CRÊPES

Prepare the master recipe as directed, stirring 1 to 2 teaspoons Mexican herb blend into the batter. Proceed as directed. On each crêpe, spread 2 to 3 tablespoons refried beans. Top with grated Monterey jack cheese, 1 to 2 tablespoons salsa, and 1 slice of avocado sprinkled with cayenne pepper, if desired. Roll up and bake as directed for stuffed crêpes in the master recipe.

APPETIZER CRÊPES

Cook the crêpes in a 9-inch skillet. When they are cool, cut each crêpe into three 3-inch rounds. On each mini crêpe, spread 1 tablespoon softened mascarpone or cream cheese. Top with either 1 blanched asparagus tip, a 3-inch sliver of smoked salmon, a halved heart of palm, or 1 marinated artichoke heart, quartered. Sprinkle with a pinch of the same flavoring as used in the crêpe batter, such as herb blend, and roll up. Serve at room temperature.

BLINI-STYLE CRÊPES

Prepare the master recipe as directed. On each crêpe, spread 1 to 2 tablespoons softened cream cheese and top with a sliver of smoked salmon or a dollop of caviar. Sprinkle with chopped fresh dill, if desired. Serve at room temperature.

MU SHU-STYLE CRÊPES

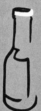

Prepare the master recipe as directed. On each crêpe, spread 1 to 2 tablespoons plum sauce or hoisin sauce, top with finely shredded cooked pork, and roll up.

PANTRY
EQUIVALENTS

BREAD

A 1-pound loaf of French bread will make 24 to 30 half-inch slices

Each slice of a 4-inch-diameter loaf of French bread will
take 2 tablespoons of sauce plus whatever else you are topping it with

PIZZA

1 cup of pasta sauce will cover a 12-inch pizza

2 ounces cheese equals $1/2$ cup grated

3 USEFUL
INFORMATION

COOKING TERMS *and* TECHNIQUES

These are the terms and techniques used throughout the book. Other methods of cooking, such as for beans, are found in the appropriate chapters.

BASTING

Brushing meats or vegetables as they roast or grill with a marinade, sauce, or other liquid helps keep them moist and adds flavor as well as color. Keep two or three sizes of pastry brushes on hand for this (and for brushing oil on a pizza crust). If you barbecue a lot, designate one just for the grill.

BLANCHING

Briefly boiling vegetables – such as broccoli, carrots, cauliflower, asparagus, or snow peas – will bring up their color and make them barely tender. Some vegetables are blanched to use in salads or to add at the end of a dish when you want more texture. To blanch, bring a pot of water to boil, drop in the vegetables, and cook for about 1 minute. Drain and set under cold running water to stop the cooking. You can also plunge the vegetables into a bowl of ice water to cool them quickly. Then drain immediately.

BROWNING

Cooking meat, poultry, or onions in a skillet in a little oil (2 tablespoons is usually fine for most ingredients) over medium-high to high heat will turn them brown to bronze and develop their flavor. This technique is often the first step in a stew or when the main ingredients will finish cooking in the oven covered with a sauce. Don't crowd the pan, or the pieces may not brown well.

CUTTING IN

In pastry making – such as for biscuits (and pie crusts) – butter or shortening is "cut in" to the flour to mix all together. The goal is to create a mixture that resembles coarse meal. Place the flour in a bowl and add the cold butter (it can be at room temperature, but the pastry won't be as flaky). Using a pastry blender, two knives, or your fingers, cut and blend the butter into the flour until it resembles a coarse meal. Work quickly if using your fingers, as the heat of your hands tends to make the butter too soft and sticky.

DEGLAZING

You can make a pan sauce after sautéing chicken, fish, or meat by deglazing. First remove the sautéed food and reserve. Drain off any excess fat. Pour a liquid such as wine, stock, water, or a sauce into the hot pan and let it sizzle. Return the pan to the heat and stir to scrape up bits of the cooked food from the bottom into the sauce. Thicken and concentrate flavor by cooking the sauce over high heat until reduced in volume. Return the chicken, fish, or meat to the pan, coat with sauce, and heat to serving temperature, or pour it over the dish to serve.

DREDGING

Put flour (seasoned, if you like) on a plate and lay the food in it to coat all over. Optionally (and this is especially good for chicken with its irregular shape), put the flour in a paper bag, drop in the food, and shake to coat all over. Coating chicken, meat, or fish in flour will help brown the food, make it crusty, and thicken a pan sauce, if there is one. Putting a little paprika in the mixture aids browning, especially when cooking skinless chicken parts.

GLAZING

A glaze is a sauce that is reduced or cooked down until it is thick and syrupy and coats the food with a shiny finish. Teriyaki is usually cooked to this point. When roasting or broiling, glaze refers to the shiny finish achieved when a meat or chicken is basted while being broiled or roasted.

GRILLING

To prepare the barbecue grill you need to build a hot fire. Never use petroleum-based fire starters – pouring vegetable oil over the coals or wood is equally successful for getting the fire started. You can use a fire-starting cone or an electric starter to speed up the process. Hardwood such as oak, hickory, madrone, or alder and natural coals of mesquite make the best cooking fire. To enhance smoky aromas, soak alder, apple, cherry, and madrone prunings or chips in water and throw them on the coals when the food is cooking.

For gas or electric grills, to approximate the smoky flavor from coals use wood chips made for them according to the manufacturer's directions.

Before putting food on the grill, always clean and oil it. A covered grill ensures the best smoky flavors.

JULIENNE

A thin-cut matchstick strip of food is called a julienne. To cut zucchini, daikon radish, or carrots, for example, into julienne, cut them into 2-inch-long pieces, then in half. Slice them lengthwise $1/8$ to $1/4$ inch thick, then cut them into matchstick-like strips $1/8$ to $1/4$ inch thick.

PEELING

Peeling and Deveining Shrimp. When a recipe directs to remove the shell of a shrimp and its dark vein, here is how to do it: Break the shell apart from the center of the underside of the shrimp, where the shell is ragged. When you get to the tail, gently break the end apart so you can retrieve the tiny tips inside, keeping a nice complete shape to the shrimp. Then, look at the other end for the black vein protruding. You can try to pull the slippery membrane out with your fingers or slice down the back of the shrimp and remove the vein.

POACHING

When food is simmered gently in nearly boiling water it cooks tender and succulent. To poach fish, chicken, vegetables, or other ingredients, bring a pot of water to boil, reduce the heat, and cook, covered or not, until done. To preserve the texture of the food, retrieve it from the water with a slotted utensil.

REDUCING

To reduce a sauce is to cook it over low to high heat to thicken it and concentrate the flavors. The lower the heat, the longer it will take. You can reduce it until it reaches any consistency from slightly thickened to a syrupy glaze.

SAUTÉING

Quickly browning and cooking chicken, meat, fish, or vegetables in a skillet is one of the quickest ways to cook something, and many complete one-skillet dinners are prepared this way. The crusty bits of food left on the bottom of the pan after cooking can be the foundation for a tasty sauce made right in the pan (see Deglazing). To sauté, warm about 2 tablespoons of oil over medium-high to high heat. Slide in the ingredients and cook as directed in a recipe, usually until softened or cooked through.

SEARING

Similar to browning, searing requires a higher heat. Searing is usually called for when you want to just brown the edges of meat that will finish cooking another way, such as braising or roasting. In a skillet over high heat, warm 1 to 2 tablespoons of oil until very hot (but not smoking!). Then slide in the steak, chop (or whatever you need to sear) to brown the outside. Turn the meat over and sear the other side.

SEEDING

Seeding Peppers. Cut the pepper in half and either with your fingers or a knife, remove the white inner part (which is usually bitter) and the seeds.

Seeding and Peeling Tomatoes. To seed, remove the stem connection from the end of the tomato. Cut the tomato in half and gently squeeze. The seeds and some of the juice will pop out. To save the juice, squeeze tomatoes into a bowl and strain the juice back into the sauce or keep for another dish.

To peel, bring a pot of water to boil. Drop in the tomatoes and boil 20 to 40 seconds, depending on their size and number. Drain, cool slightly, and peel off the skin, which is already popping off from the dip in hot water.

SIMMERING

A simmering liquid just slightly bubbles over medium to medium-low heat; it is less than a full boil. This is a gentle way to get food tender. The pan may be covered or not.

SKINNING

Skinning Chicken. Removing poultry skin is a surprisingly easy process. All you need are your fingers and a small knife. For the breasts and thighs insert your fingers between the skin and meat and pull the skin away. Where it resists, cut it off. For the drumsticks, pull the skin down toward the knobby end (holding onto the skin with a paper towel helps), then pull it completely off, as if removing a sock. Also remove the fat pockets with your knife.

TOASTING

Toasting Nuts and Seeds. Toasting brings up the flavor of nuts and seeds for any use. Preheat the oven to 350 degrees F. Spread walnuts, almonds, hazelnuts, pecans, pine nuts, sesame seeds, or other nuts or seeds on a rimmed baking sheet. Toast in the oven 5 to 15 minutes, depending on the size and quantity. When near done, you will smell a nutty aroma. Remove and cool before using.

ZESTING

The outer, colored part of the peel of citrus fruits such as oranges, lemons, and limes is the zest. To remove this aromatic ingredient for use in cooking, gently rub the citrus on a grater (try not to grate the inner white pith, which has a bitter flavor). Or use a zester, which has tiny sharp holes designed to remove only the flavorful essence of citrus peels.

SOURCES

Many of these companies have mail order; call or write for catalog.

ASIAN PASTES AND SAUCES

Cinnabar Specialty Foods
1134 West Haining Street
Prescott, Arizona 86301
520-778-3687

A wide range of Indian curry sauces
and pastes and chutneys; plus jerk
and other Caribbean sauces

**East India Spice Company/
Instant India**
P.O. Box 2010
Cambridge, Massachusetts 02238
617-868-3539

Indian curry and other sauces

Epicurean International
P.O. Box 13242
Berkeley, California 94701
510-268-0209

Gourmet America
350 Lincoln Street
Hingham, Massachusetts 02043
800-352-1352; 617-749-6132

Patak brand Indian curry sauces and
Inner Beauty Caribbean, fish, and
barbecue sauces

Lee Kum Kee
P.O. Box 6338
304 South Date Avenue
Alhambra, California 91803
800-654-5082; 818-282-0337

Stir-fry, black bean, and other
Chinese sauces

Rajah/Victoria's Treasure
9930 Pioneer Boulevard #10
Sante Fe Springs, California 90670
800-448-8832; 310-942-2433

Masala, minced ginger, tandoor
paste, curry paste

Soy Vay Enterprises
P.O. Box 410671
San Francisco, California
94141-0671
800-600-2077

Kosher teriyaki and other marinades

Sukhi's
1933 Davis Street, Suite 284
San Leandro, California 94577
510-633-1144

Curry paste, tandoori marinade,
masalas, chutney

New World Spices
160 Ellis Street
San Francisco, California 94102
415-399-9799

Large selection of Indian curry and
other dried seasonings and blends

Penzeys, Ltd. Spice House
P.O. Box 1448
Waukesha, Wisconsin 53187
414-574-0277

Dried spice and herb blends such
as Latin American adobo, barbecue
rub, bouquet garni, Bavarian, fajita,
tandoori, vindaloo, curry, jerk,
salad seasonings, shrimp and crab
boil; plus filé, saffron, annatto, and
whole ginger

**Sadaf International
Gourmet Foods**
2828 South Alameda Street
Los Angeles, California 90058
800-852-4050

Fish and shish-kabob seasoning

SoHo Provisions
(see Vinegars and Oils, page 254)

Southern Ray's
(see Barbecue Sauces, Marinades,
and Glazes, page 246)

The Spice Hunter
San Luis Obispo, California 93401
800-444-3061

Large selection of herb and
spice blends

Spiceland
3206 North Major Avenue
Chicago, Illinois 60634
800-352-8671; 312-736-1217

Every spice and blend you can think
of, and inexpensive!

Starport
30560 San Antonio Street
Hayward, California 94544
510-441-9601

Roasted garlic, cilantro, basil, and
chile olive oils; Cajun, Italian,
Mexican seasoning blends; jerk
and barbecue rubs; Carnival del
Sol sauces

Vanns Spices Ltd.
1238 East Joppa Road
Baltimore, Maryland 21286
800-583-1693; 410-583-1643

Fish, Cajun blackened, island jerk,
and herbes de Provence herb blends

Vitasoy Inc.
400 Oyster Point Boulevard,
Suite 201
South San Francisco, California
94080
800-VITASOY; 415-583-9888

TofuMate herb blends

BOULLION AND STOCK

Chef Piero Biondi
5900 San Fernando Road
Glendale, California 91202-2797
213-245-2388; 818-244-8483

Beef, chicken, veal stock
concentrates

Burton and Company
6613 Hollis Street
Emeryville, California 94608
510-652-0101

Vegetable and herb stocks

More Than Gourmet
800/860-9385; 330-762-6652

Chicken, veal, and vegetarian stock
concentrates

Perfect Addition
Box 8976
Newport Beach, California 92658-89764
714/640-0220

Chicken, veal, meat stock
concentrates

CHUTNEYS AND RELISHES

Alexander Valley Fruit & Trading Company
5110 Highway 128
Geyserville, CA 95441
800-433-1944; 707/433-1944

Mustard, barbecue, chutney, and
other sauces and pastes

American Spoon
(see Barbecue Sauces, Marinades,
and Glazes, page 245)

Cinnabar Specialty Foods
(see Asian Pastes and Sauces,
page 244)

Drummond Farms Fresh Fruit Chutneys
P.O. Box 1694
Mendocino, California 95460
707-937-1758

Pear, raspberry, ginger, and other
fresh fruit chutneys

Gloria's Sample & Company
199 East Avenue
Lake Oswego, Oregon 97034
800-782-5881; 503-636-3520

Apple and banana chutneys, catsup

Hot Pepper Jelly Company
330 North Main Street
Fort Bragg, California 95437
800-892-4823; 707-961-1422

Pepper jellies, salad dressing, mustard, pepper vinegar, chutney, herb
and spice blends

Taste of Israel
Greater Galilee Gourmet
2118 Wilshire Boulevard, Suite 829
Santa Monica, California 90403
800-290-1391

Za'atar pesto, marinade, and spice;
tahini; hot and sour garlic sauce,
and more

Timber Crest Farms
(see Chutneys and Relishes,
page 249)

Todaro Bros.
(see Pasta Sauces, page 251)

Victoria Packing Corporation
(see Pasta Sauces, page 252)

Vivande Porta Via
(see Vinegars and Oils, page 254)

World Variety Produce, Inc.
Melissa's Brand
P.O. Box 21127
Los Angeles, California 90021
800-588-0151

Roasted bell peppers, crushed ginger, pesto, stir-fry seasoning, salsa,
chopped garlic, pine nuts

SALAD DRESSINGS

American Spoon
(see Barbecue Sauces, Marinades,
and Glazes, page 245)

Judyth's Mountain
(see Chutneys and Relishes,
page 249)

Kozlowski Farms
(see Barbecue Sauces, Marinades,
and Glazes, page 245)

Oak Hill Farms
(see Barbecue Sauces, Marinades,
and Glazes, page 246)

The Silver Palate
(see Chutneys and Relishes,
page 249)

VINEGARS AND OILS

Cuisine Perel
3100 Kerner Boulevard
San Rafael, California 94901
415-456-4406

Infused grapeseed oils; chile-, garlic-,
and artichoke-flavored dried pasta

Fetzer Vineyards
P.O. Box 333
Hopland, California 95449
800-959-5035

Flavored vinegars, sun-dried
tomatoes

Hot Pepper Jelly Company
(see Chutneys and Relishes, page 248)

Judyth's Mountain
(see Chutneys and Relishes, page 249)

Katz and Company
6770 Washington Street
Yountville, California 94599
800-455-2305

Flavored vinegars, olive oil, mustards

Kennedy Gourmet
1313 Energy Drive
Kilgore, Texas 75662
800-657-5258; 903-896-3227

Large line of infused oils and vinegars; pasta sauces; pastas; barbecue sauces; and dried garlic and pasta sauce seasonings

Kozlowski Farms
(see Barbecue Sauces, Marinades, and Glazes, page 245)

Loriva Supreme Foods
20 Oser Avenue
Hauppauge, New York 11788
800-94-LORIVA

Sesame, walnut, olive, and other oils

**Napa Valley Kitchens/
Consorzio Brand**
4 Financial Plaza
Napa, California 94558
800-288-1089

Roasted garlic, porcini mushrooms, basil, and five-pepper olive oils; roasted garlic paste; salad dressings; pasta and rice

Navarro Vineyards
P.O. Box 147
Philo, California 95466
707-895-3686

Verjus

SoHo Provisions
International Foods
518 Broadway
New York, New York 10012
212-334-4311

Dried spices, oils and vinegars, rice, grains, mustards, hot sauces, and other seasonings from around the world

Urban Herbs
18911 Premiere Court
Gaithersburg, Maryland 20879
800-77 HERBS; 301-330-5809

Basil, Italian, Santa Fe flavored vinegars; dried tomatoes; infused oils

Vivande Porta Via
2125 Fillmore Street
San Francisco, California 94115

Olive paste, roasted peppers, pesto, saffron, sun-dried tomato paste, truffle paste, pastas, olive oils, vinegars, truffle oil

Cuisine Perel
3100 Kerner Boulevard
San Rafael, California 94901
415-456-4406

Flavored and whimsically
shaped pastas

Dean & DeLuca
560 Broadway
New York, New York 10012
212-431-1691

Pasta, polenta, beans, rice

Elite Foods
489 Cabot Road
San Francisco, California 94080
800-376-5368; 415-871-0826

Shelf-stable polenta

Ferrara Food Co.
120 Tices Lane, Suite C
Brunswick, New Jersey 08816-2014
908-651-7600

Assorted pastas, instant polenta,
beans, risotto, roasted peppers

Todaro Brothers
555 Second Avenue
New York, New York 10016
212-679-7766

Variety of pastas, rices, beans,
couscous, dried mushrooms, truffles

Vigo Importing Company
4701 West Comanche Avenue
Tampa, Florida 33614
813-884-3491

Alessi brand pastas, dried
mushrooms

Vivande Porta Via
(see Vinegars and Oils, page 254)

Polenta, pastas, olive oil

Williams-Sonoma
P.O. Box 7456
San Francisco, California
94120-7456
800-541-2233

Pastas, rices

World Variety Produce, Inc.
(see Pastes and Pestos, page 253)

Couscous; rice; crepes; dried
mushrooms, chiles, beans; marinated
artichokes, roated peppers,
crushed ginger

Zabar's
2245 Broadway (at 80th Street)
New York, New York 10024
212-496-1234

Pastas, condiments

BIBLIOGRAPHY

Brennan, Jennifer. *The Cuisines of Asia. New York:* St. Martin's Press, 1984.

Chiarello, Michael, with Penelope Wisner. *Flavored Vinegars.* San Francisco: Chronicle Books, 1996.

Cost, Bruce. *Bruce Cost's Asian Ingredients.* New York: William Morrow and Company, Inc., 1988.

Cusumano, Camille. *Tofu, Tempeh, and Other Soy Delights.* Emmaus, Pennsylvania: Rodale Press, 1984.

Ettlinger, Steve, with Melanie Falick. *The Restaurant Lover's Companion.* Reading, Massachusetts: Addison-Wesley Publishing Company, 1995.

Hazen, Janet. *Mustard: Making Your Own Gourmet Mustards.* San Francisco: Chronicle Books, 1993.

Kondo, Sonoko. *The Poetical Pursuit of Food: Japanese Recipes for American Cooks.* New York: Clarkson Potter, Inc., Publishers, 1986.

Law, Ruth. *The Southeast Asia Cookbook.* New York: Primus, Donald I. Fine, Inc., 1995.

Mallos, Tess. *The Complete Middle East Cookbook.* New York: McGraw-Hill Book Company, 1986.

Norman, Jill. *Spices, Seeds, and Barks.* New York: Bantam Books, 1990.

Rozin, Elisabeth. *Ethnic Cuisine: The Flavor Principle Cookbook.* Lexington, Massachusetts: The Stephen Greene Press, 1983.

Sananikone, Keo. *Keo's Thai Cuisine.* Berkeley: Ten Speed Press, 1986.

Spieler, Marlena. *From Pantry to Table: Creative Cooking from the Well-stocked Kitchen.* Reading, Massachusetts: Aris Books, Addison-Wesley Publishing Company, Inc., 1991.